Decorate It!

Publications International, Ltd.

Front cover photography by:
Photography: Stephen Hamilton Photographics, Inc.
Photographer: Stephen Hamilton
Photographer's Assistant: Lisa Predko
Food Stylist: Lois Hlavac
Assistant Food Stylist: Susie Skoog

Pictured on the front cover *(clockwise from top left)*: Chocolate Midnight Cake *(page 66)*, Chocolate Curls *(page 21)*, Orange Rose *(page 24)*, Cookie Fruit *(page 46)*, Strawberry Fan *(page 14)*, Cherry Cheese Pie *(page 83)*, Candied Citrus Peel *(page 19)*, Double-Dipped Chocolate Peanut Butter Cookies *(page 42)*, Swiss Mocha Treats *(page 33)* and Sugared Fruit *(page 14)*.

Pictured on the back cover *(clockwise from top left)*: Back-To-School Pencil Cake *(page 67)*, Apple Cider Cake *(page 70)*, Rainbows *(page 43)* and Jolly Peanut Butter Gingerbread Cookies *(page 126)*.

ISBN: 0-7853-3548-X

Library of Congress Catalog Card Number: 99-74127

Manufactured in China.

8 7 6 5 4 3 2 1

Microwave Cooking: Microwave ovens vary in wattage. Use the cooking times as guidelines and check for doneness before adding more time.

CONTENTS

DECORATE IT!

tips & techniques

Decorating food turns an ordinary event into a celebration. When you know the tricks of the trade, it's easy. The following tips and techniques will help you create food that looks good enough to eat!

BACK TO BASICS

No matter what you're preparing, beautiful food starts with good cooking basics. Here are some guidelines to keep in mind when you're ready to start the fun in the kitchen.

• Before beginning, read the entire recipe to make sure you have all the necessary ingredients, utensils and supplies.

• For best results, use the ingredients called for in the recipe. Butter, margarine and shortening are not always interchangeable.

• Follow the recipe directions and cooking or baking times exactly. Check for doneness using the test given in the recipe.

• Always use the pan or dish size specified in each recipe. Using a different size pan or dish may cause under or overcooking, or sticking and burnt edges.

A PIECE OF CAKE

Not everybody has the experience to decorate like a pro, but with these simple hints, anyone can decorate a cake with professional looking results.

• To get a more professional look, trim off the rounded top of the cake. Use a serrated knife long enough to cut across the top in one stroke, such as a bread knife. Cut through the cake horizontally using a gentle sawing motion. If necessary, the sides of square or rectangular cakes can also be trimmed to make them more even.

• If making layers, cut the cake horizontally in half or in thirds, using the same technique for trimming the top of the cake as directed above.

• Before frosting the cake, brush off all loose cake crumbs with a soft pastry brush.

• Place the cake on a serving plate or covered cake board before frosting it. To keep the plate or board clean, simply tuck strips of waxed paper under the edges of the cake, then frost. When you are finished decorating, gently slide the waxed paper out from under the cake. Then add any final decorations around the base of the cake.

CAKE BOARDS

Some cakes are too large or oddly shaped for standard plates and platters. Use cake boards, cutting boards, cookie sheets or other large flat surfaces. Cake boards are made of sturdy cardboard and are available in round or rectangular shapes of various sizes. They can usually be found in craft and kitchenware stores. Cake boards can be covered with foil, greaseproof paper, paper doilies or plastic wrap. To cover, cut the foil or paper 1 to 2 inches larger than the board. Center the board on the reverse side of the paper. Cut slashes in the paper almost to the board along any curved edges. Fold the edges over the board and tape into place. If a cake is very heavy, stack two cake boards together before covering for additional support.

IT'S IN THE BAG

When decorating with a decorating bag (also called a pastry bag), a coupler can make changing tips much easier. A coupler is used to attach tips to the decorating bag and allows you to change tips without removing the frosting from the bag. To use, unscrew the ring.

Insert the cone-shaped piece into the narrow end of an empty decorating bag until the narrow end extends slightly beyond the end of the bag (snip off the end of the decorating bag if necessary). Place the coupler ring over the decorating tip. Screw the ring on to hold the tip in place. To change tips, unscrew the ring, remove the tip, replace with the new tip and screw the ring back in place.

DECORATE IT!

To fill a decorating bag, insert the tip or attach it with a coupler. Fold the top of the bag down and place the frosting in the bag. In general, fill the bag half to two-thirds full, then unfold the top of the bag. Twist the top of the bag tightly against the frosting.

Place the twisted end of the bag in the palm of your writing hand with fingers positioned near the bag opening. Place your other hand under the bag to guide the tip as shown.

When piping, hold the bag so the tip is at the angle indicated for the technique. Then, gently squeeze the bag from the top, using even pressure while guiding the tip with your other hand. Squeeze mainly with the palm of your hand rather than your fingers. Be careful not to loosen your grip on the twisted end or the frosting will begin to push up and out of the top of the bag.

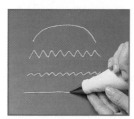

Line (use writing or small open star tip): Hold bag so tip is at a 45° angle to the right. While gently squeezing bag, guide tip opening just above cake in a curved, zigzag, squiggly or straight line. To end line, stop squeezing, then lift tip.

Writing (use writing tip): Hold bag so tip is at a 45° angle to the right for horizontal lines and toward you for vertical lines. While gently squeezing bag, guide tip opening just above cake to form print or script letters. Stop squeezing, then lift tip at the end of each letter for print letters and at the end of each word for script writing.

Dot (use round tip): Hold bag so tip is at a 90° angle. Position opening just above the cake and gently squeeze. Lift slightly while still squeezing. When dot is desired size, stop squeezing, then lift tip. To pipe a dot border, position tip almost touching first dot and pipe another dot. Repeat to complete border.

Shell (use round tip, or open or closed star tip): Hold bag so tip is at a 45° angle to the right just above the cake. Squeeze until a small mound is formed for base of shell, lifting slightly. Keep pulling tip away from base to the right until tail is desired length. Stop squeezing, then lift tip. To pipe a shell border, position tip almost touching tail of first shell and pipe another shell. Repeat to complete border.

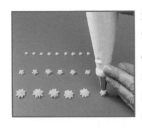

Star (use open or closed star tip): Hold bag so tip is at a 90° angle. Position opening just above the cake and gently squeeze. Lift slightly while still squeezing. When star is desired size, stop squeezing, then lift tip. To pipe a star border, position tip almost touching first star and pipe another star. Repeat to complete border.

PICTURE PERFECT PIES

Any pie can be pretty as a picture using one of these decorative crusts.

Cutouts: Trim edge of bottom crust even with pie plate. Cut desired shapes from remaining pastry using tiny cookie cutter. Moisten pastry edge. Place cutouts on pastry edge, slightly overlapping. Press into place.

Fork Edge: Trim edge of bottom crust even with pie plate. Press to rim of pie plate using 4-tined fork. Leave about 1¼ inches between marks. Go around crust edge again, filling in spaces with fork held at an angle.

Pinwheel: Fold overhang of bottom crust under; press flat. Cut slits around edge of pastry the width of the pie plate rim, leaving about 1 inch between slits. Fold under on a diagonal to form pinwheel points.

Rope Edge: Fold overhang of bottom crust under and stand edge up. Press thumb into pastry at an angle. Pinch pastry between thumb and knuckle of index finger, rolling knuckle towards thumb. Place thumb in groove left by finger and continue around edge.

Gelatin/Chocolate Cutouts

2 (4-serving size) packages of cherry, orange or lime gelatin
1 envelope unflavored gelatin
1½ cups cranberry or apple juice
Semisweet chocolate (for chocolate cutouts), shaved or chopped
Shortening (for chocolate cutouts)

1. For gelatin cutouts, place gelatin in bowl. Pour juice into saucepan. Bring to a boil. Gradually add hot juice to gelatin, stirring with spoon until gelatin is dissolved. Cool to room temperature.

2. Line baking pan with plastic wrap, leaving enough wrap to extend over edges. Slowly pour in dissolved gelatin; chill until firm.

3. Using plastic wrap, carefully lift gelatin from pan; place on cutting board. Cut gelatin into desired shapes with cookie cutters, placing cutters as close together as possible. Carefully remove cutouts with metal spatula. Place on desired food or plate.

4. For chocolate cutouts, place chocolate in measuring cup. Add shortening. (Use 1 teaspoon shortening for every 2 ounces chocolate.) Fill saucepan one-quarter full (about 1 inch deep) with warm (not hot) water. Place measuring cup in water to melt chocolate, stirring frequently until smooth. (Be careful not to get any water into chocolate.) Remove measuring cup from saucepan. Let chocolate cool slightly.

5. Line baking sheet with waxed paper. Pour melted chocolate onto prepared baking sheet; quickly spread chocolate into thin layer (⅛ to ¼ inch thick). Let stand in cool, dry place until chocolate is just firm. (Do not chill in refrigerator.)

6. Cut chocolate into shapes with cookie cutters, placing cutters as close together as possible. Carefully remove cutouts. Store in cool, dry place until ready to use.

Tip: *For ease in cutting chocolate cutouts, slightly warm cookie cutters in your hands before cutting.*

Clockwise from top left: Gelatin/Chocolate Cutouts, Feathered Icing (page 12), Gumdrop Bow (page 15), Chocolate Leaves (page 19) and Caramel Roses (page 18).

Feathered Sauces/Icings

Desired sauce or icing
Desired sauce, melted chocolate or icing of contrasting color
Cake, brownies or cookies

SUPPLIES
Decorating bag or parchment cone and small writing tip

1. For feathered sauces, spoon desired sauce onto individual dessert plates. Tilt plate to spread sauce evenly.

2. Use spoon or decorating bag fitted with writing tip to drizzle contrasting sauce in evenly spaced parallel lines or spiral design over sauce on plate. Feather by drawing knife through parallel lines in same direction at regular intervals or for spiral design, from outside to center. For a different look, alternate direction in which knife is drawn through lines or spiral.

3. For feathered icings, spread desired icing over a cake or cookies. If using parchment cone, cut about ½ inch off bottom point of cone. Position writing tip in opening of decorating bag or parchment cone. (If necessary, cut larger opening in parchment to get tip to fit.) Fill bag or cone about half full with contrasting icing. Squeeze down from open end of bag or cone.

4. Place open end of bag or cone in palm of writing hand. Position fingers near bag opening or near cone tip. Place other hand under bag or cone. Hold bag or cone at 45° angle just above food. While gently squeezing bag, guide tip to pipe line across top of iced cake. At end of line, stop squeezing and then lift bag. Repeat to pipe parallel lines. Or pipe one line in spiral design.

5. Holding knife at right angle to parallel lines, draw knife through lines at regular intervals, pulling utensil in the same direction. For spiral design, pull knife from outside to center. For a different look, alternate direction in which knife is drawn through lines or spiral.

Step 2: Draw knife in alternate direction through spiral.

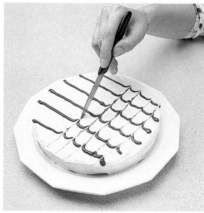

Step 3: Draw knife in same direction through lines.

Lime/Lemon Wedges

1 lime or lemon, cut in half lengthwise

1. Place fruit half, cut side down, on cutting board. Working in center of top of fruit, cut out thin, shallow wedge from fruit, being careful not to cut all the way into fruit. Remove wedge; set aside.

2. Using gentle sawing motion, continue cutting progressively larger wedges (each ⅛ inch larger than last) for total of four or five wedges. Remove each wedge as it is cut.

3. Repeat with remaining half of fruit.

Serving Suggestion: For an easy yet elegant dessert, place scoops of lime sherbet in pretty glasses; trim each serving with a lime or lemon wedge and a sprig of mint. Arrange two or three lime or lemon wedges in the center of a key lime or other citrus-based cream pie. Perk up a bowl of buttered rice or rice pilaf with a lemon wedge garnish.

Bell Pepper Triangles

Green, red and/or yellow bell pepper
Bowl of ice water (optional)

1. Stand bell pepper, stem side up, on cutting board. Cut slice, about ¼ inch thick, off each side of pepper. Remove membrane and seeds; discard.

2. Cut each pepper slice into rectangle 1¼ inches long and ¾ inch wide. Starting one-third of the way from one long side of each rectangle, cut down remaining length of rectangle, ending ¼ inch from other end. Turn rectangle around; repeat on other side.

3. To make each triangle, hold the two outer corners of a rectangle and bring both corners to center. Overlap ends to secure. If desired, place triangles in ice water to crispen. Remove; drain well.

Scored Citrus Slices

Lemon, lime, orange or grapefruit
SUPPLIES
Citrus stripper or grapefruit spoon

1. Cut groove in peel of fruit with citrus stripper or tip of grapefruit spoon, cutting lengthwise from stem end to other end.

2. Continue to cut grooves about ¼ to ½ inch apart completely around fruit.

3. Cut fruit crosswise into thin slices.

Helpful Hint

When choosing a garnish, pick one that enhances and complements the color and texture of the food. Use a bright garnish to perk up a light-colored food. Accent a soft-textured food with a crisp garnish. For example, crispy and colorful bell pepper triangles can add excitement to grilled meats.

Sugared Fruit/Flowers

Grapes (in small clusters), cranberries, bing cherries and/or blueberries
Egg white*
Granulated sugar
Fresh small edible flowers such as geraniums, roses, nasturtiums, violets and marigolds
Superfine sugar

SUPPLIES
Small nontoxic leaves (optional)
Small, clean paintbrush or pastry brush

Use only grade A clean, uncracked eggs.

1. For sugared fruit, wash fruit. Gently blot dry with paper towels or let air-dry on paper towels.

2. Beat egg white in small bowl until foamy. Brush egg white onto each piece of fruit with paintbrush or pastry brush, coating all sides of fruit thinly and evenly.

3. Place fruit on waxed paper that has been covered with sugar. Sprinkle light, even coating of sugar over fruit. If any areas are not coated, repeat layers of egg white and sugar. Let sugared fruit stand at room temperature until coating is dry. Trim with nontoxic leaves, if desired.

4. For sugared flowers, substitute edible flowers for fruit and superfine sugar for granulated sugar. Wash flowers. Gently blot dry with paper towels or let air-dry on paper towels.

5. Beat egg white in small bowl with fork until foamy. Brush egg white onto each flower with paintbrush, coating both sides of petals thinly and evenly.

6. Place flower on large sheet of waxed paper that has been covered with sugar. Spoon additional sugar into sieve. Sift light, even coating of sugar over each flower. If any areas are not coated, repeat layers of egg white and sugar. Let sugared flowers stand at room temperature until coating is dry.

Strawberry Fans

Strawberries with tops attached

1. Place strawberry on cutting board with pointed end facing you. Make four or five lengthwise cuts from just below stem end of strawberry to pointed end.

2. Fan slices apart slightly, being careful to keep all slices attached to cap. Place on plate or food.

Cucumber/Citrus Twists

1 small cucumber, ends trimmed *or* 1 citrus fruit

Diagonally cut cucumber or citrus fruit into thin slices. Cut slit through each slice just to center. Holding each slice with both hands, twist ends in opposite directions. Place on plate or desired food to secure.

Gumdrop Bow

Sugar
8 to 10 small gumdrops

1. Sprinkle sugar on cutting board. Flatten gumdrops. Place gumdrops, with ends overlapping slightly, on sugared board in two rows of four to five gumdrops each. Sprinkle gumdrops with additional sugar.

2. Roll flattened gumdrops into a 6✕3-inch piece with rolling pin, turning strip over frequently to coat with sugar. Trim and discard edges of gumdrop piece. Cut remaining piece into ½-inch-wide strips.

3. Cut two 3-inch lengths, four 2½-inch lengths and one 1½-inch length from strips.

4. To assemble bow, fold both 3-inch lengths in half to form two loops; place end to end to form base of bow. Press ends together to secure. Fold over two of the 2½-inch lengths; place end to end on top of first loops, pressing gently to secure. Wrap 1½-inch length crosswise around center of bow to conceal ends of loops. Press gently to secure.

5. Trim ends of remaining two 2½-inch lengths at angle. Place these lengths under center of bow in upside-down "V" to make ends of bow. Press gently to attach to bow.

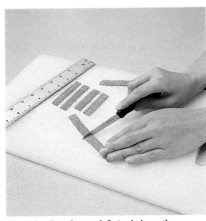

Step 3: Cut 2- and 3-inch lengths.

Step 4: Press gently to secure.

Chocolate-Dipped Delights

1 cup chopped toasted almonds
1⅔ cups (about 10 ounces) chopped white chocolate
2 cups (about 12 ounces) chopped semisweet chocolate
1⅔ cups (about 10 ounces) chopped milk chocolate
3 tablespoons shortening, divided
Heart-shaped pretzels
Biscotti
Sandwich cookies
Ridged potato chips

SUPPLIES
Small, clean paintbrush or pastry brush

1. Place nuts in medium bowl. Set aside. To melt chocolate, place each kind of chocolate and 1 tablespoon shortening in separate 4-cup glass measuring cups. Microwave, 1 measuring cup at a time, at MEDIUM (50% power) 4 to 5 minutes or until chocolate is melted, stirring after 2 minutes.

2. Place large sheet waxed paper on counter. Dip ½ of each pretzel into white chocolate. Gently shake off excess chocolate; place on waxed paper. Let stand 10 minutes; repeat. Let stand 30 minutes or until set.

3. Dip other halves of pretzels into semisweet chocolate. Place on waxed paper. Let stand until set.

4. Spread milk chocolate on curved edge of biscotti with small knife. Roll in nuts. Place on waxed paper. Let stand 30 minutes or until set.

5. Holding sandwich cookie flat, dip 1 side of each cookie into semisweet chocolate. Shake off excess chocolate. Place on waxed paper. Let stand 30 minutes or until set. Repeat with second side.

6. To paint potato chips, dip small paint brush into milk chocolate. Paint chocolate onto 1 side of each chip. Let stand 30 minutes or until set.

7. Store loosely covered at room temperature up to 1 week.

Makes 3 cups melted chocolate

Tasty Tidbit

Toasting nuts brings out their flavor and gives them a wonderful golden color. To toast nuts, spread them in a single layer on a baking sheet. Bake in a 325°F oven 8 to 10 minutes or until golden. Stir nuts occasionally during baking to ensure even toasting. The nuts will darken and become crisper as they cool.

Chocolate-Dipped Delights

Caramel Rose

Sugar
3 purchased caramels, unwrapped

1. Sprinkle some sugar on cutting board. Place caramels on sugared board. Sprinkle with additional sugar. Roll each caramel into an oval (about 1/16 inch thick) with rolling pin, turning oval over frequently to coat with sugar. Cut each oval in half crosswise.

2. To make center of rose, start at one side of half oval and roll up to form bud shape. To make petals, shape another half oval, straight side down, around bud. Press petal to bud to secure; flare top edge slightly to resemble petal. Repeat with remaining half ovals to shape additional petals, overlapping petals slightly. Place rose on its side; trim off base so rose will sit flat. ***Makes 1 rose***

Step 2: Shape another half oval around bud.

Step 2: Repeat with remaining half ovals.

Green Onion/Celery Curls

Green onion or celery rib
Bowl of cold water (for green onion curl)
Bowl of ice water (for celery curl)

1. For green onion curl, cut off and discard roots from green onion. Cut onion crosswise into one 3-inch piece, leaving about 1½ inches of both white and green portions.

2. Using the tip of sharp knife, cut white end of onion lengthwise almost to center into very thin strips. Place onion in cold water (not ice water). Let stand 30 seconds or until ends curl slightly. Remove from water; drain well.

3. For celery curl, trim ends from celery rib; cut into 3-inch pieces. Cut each piece lengthwise in half. Cut into slivers as directed in step 2 above. Place in ice water and refrigerate until ends curl.

Chocolate Leaves

Semisweet chocolate (squares or bars), shaved or chopped
Shortening
SUPPLIES
Nontoxic leaves, such as rose, lemon or camellia
Small, clean paintbrush or pastry brush

1. Place chocolate in measuring cup. Add shortening. (Use 1 teaspoon shortening for every 2 ounces chocolate.) Fill saucepan one-quarter full (about 1 inch deep) with warm (not hot) water. Place measuring cup in water to melt chocolate, stirring frequently until smooth. (Be careful not to get any water into chocolate.) Remove measuring cup from saucepan. Let chocolate cool slightly.

2. Wash leaves; dry well with paper towels. Brush melted chocolate onto underside of each leaf with paintbrush or pastry brush, coating leaf thickly and evenly. Repeat brushing with second coating of chocolate, if desired, for sturdier leaf. Carefully wipe off any chocolate that may have run onto front of leaf.

3. Place leaves, chocolate side up, on waxed paper. Let stand in cool, dry place until chocolate is firm. (Do not chill in refrigerator.)

4. When chocolate is firm, carefully peel leaves away from chocolate; chill until ready to use.

Candied Citrus Peel

1 lime, lemon, orange or grapefruit
1½ cups sugar plus additional
1½ cups water

1. Wash fruit; dry thoroughly with paper towels. Cut peel from fruit with vegetable peeler. If necessary, scrape cut side of peel to remove white membrane. Cut peel into very thin strips.

2. Combine sugar and water in small saucepan. Bring to a boil over medium heat, stirring constantly with wooden spoon. Boil 3 minutes.

3. Carefully add peel strips to boiling mixture. Reduce heat to low. Simmer 10 to 12 minutes or until peel turns completely translucent.

4. Place wire strainer or sieve over bowl. Spoon peel strips into strainer; drain thoroughly. Add additional sugar to resealable plastic food storage bag. Add peel strips; seal bag. Shake until evenly coated with sugar. Remove strips from bag; place on waxed paper to dry thoroughly.

Helpful Hint

Garnishes don't have to be elaborate. For example, a sprinkle of chopped fresh herbs or tomatoes can add color to a casserole or side dish. Or, a delicate spray of edible flowers can make an attractive presentation on anything from a savory vegetable dip to a fluffy-frosted birthday cake.

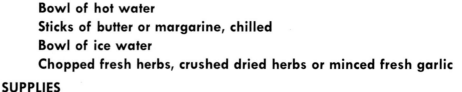

Butter Shapes

Bowl of hot water
Sticks of butter or margarine, chilled
Bowl of ice water
Chopped fresh herbs, crushed dried herbs or minced fresh garlic

SUPPLIES
Butter curler (for butter curls)
Butter paddles (for butter balls)
Small candy molds (for molded butter)
Shaped butter dishes or other small dishes (for butter pots)

1. For butter curls, place butter curler in hot water. Starting at far end of one butter stick, pull curler firmly across top. Place finished curl in ice water. Repeat for desired amount of curls, dipping curler into hot water before starting each curl.

2. For butter balls, place butter paddles in ice water until cold. Place one butter stick on cutting board; cut into ½-inch pieces. Shape pieces into balls. Chill until firm, if necessary. Roll each ball between scored sides of paddles, moving paddles in small circles in opposite directions. Place finished butter balls in ice water.

3. For molded butter, allow one butter stick to stand at room temperature until softened. Place candy mold in ice water until cold. Press butter firmly and evenly into mold; level top with knife. Chill until butter is firm. Gently remove molded butter from candy mold using tip of knife. Place finished molded butter in ice water until ready to serve.

4. For individual butter pots, allow one butter stick to stand at room temperature until softened. Press butter firmly and evenly into shaped dishes; smooth top with metal spatula or back of teaspoon. Make decorative crisscross markings across tops with fork or knife, if desired.

5. For seasoned butter, allow one butter stick to stand at room temperature until softened. Place butter in small bowl. Add herbs or garlic; stir until well blended. (Use about 1 teaspoon fresh herbs or ¼ to ½ teaspoon dried herbs or minced garlic for each stick butter.) Place butter mixture on waxed paper; shape into roll. Wrap with waxed paper; chill until firm. To serve, slice butter roll into rounds. Or, use seasoned butter roll to make butter curls or balls.

Chocolate Curls

Semisweet chocolate (squares or bars), chopped
Shortening

1. Place chocolate in measuring cup; add shortening. (Use 1 teaspoon shortening for every 2 ounces chocolate.) Fill saucepan one-quarter full (about 1 inch deep) with warm (not hot) water.

2. Place measuring cup in water to melt chocolate, stirring frequently until smooth. (Be careful not to get any water into chocolate.) Remove measuring cup from saucepan. Let chocolate cool slightly.

3. Pour melted chocolate onto back of baking pan. Quickly spread chocolate into thin layer (about ¼ inch thick).

4. Let chocolate stand in cool, dry place until firm. (Do not chill in refrigerator.) When chocolate is just firm, use small metal pancake turner to form curls. Hold pancake turner at 45° angle and scrape chocolate into curl. Using toothpick, transfer curl to waxed paper. Store in cool, dry place until ready to use.

Pastry Cutouts

All-purpose flour
Pastry for pie crust
Milk
Sugar
Water

1. Lightly flour surface and rolling pin. Roll out dough to about ⅛-inch thickness. (To minimize pastry sticking to rolling pin, use rolling pin with cloth cover.) Cut into desired shapes using small cookie cutters or knife.

2. To decorate baked single-crust pie, transfer pastry cutouts to baking sheet. Use tip of knife to decorate cutouts with design, if desired. Brush cutouts with milk; sprinkle with sugar.

3. Bake cutouts at 425°F (or at temperature given in pastry recipe) until golden brown. Transfer to wire rack; cool. Arrange baked cutouts on top of pie filling.

4. To decorate unbaked double-crust pie, remove cutouts from pastry cloth. Brush back side of cutouts with water. Arrange cutouts, moistened side down, on top crust of pie.

5. Cut slits in top pie crust as part of design. Or, cut slits along edge of cutouts. Brush crust and cutouts with milk; sprinkle with sugar. Bake as directed in pie recipe.

Piped Cream Cheese

Whipped cream cheese
Fresh dill

1. Fill resealable plastic food storage bag about half full with cream cheese. Seal bag securely. Cut small piece off bottom corner of bag. Place sealed end in writing hand. Position fingers near opening of bag; place other hand under bag.

2. For squiggles and lines, hold plastic bag at 45° angle about ¼ inch from surface of food. While gently squeezing bag, guide bag to create desired design. At end of each squiggle or line, stop squeezing bag and lift away from food. Garnish with fresh dill.

3. For puffs and dollops, hold plastic bag at 90° angle. Position opening just above food and gently squeeze, lifting bag slightly while squeezing. When puff or dollop is desired size, stop squeezing and lift up bag. Garnish with fresh dill.

Chocolate Drizzles/Shapes

Semisweet or milk chocolate (squares or bars), shaved or chopped

1. Place shavings in measuring cup. Fill saucepan one-quarter full (about 1 inch deep) with warm (not hot) water. Place measuring cup in water to melt chocolate, stirring frequently until smooth. (Be careful not to get any water into chocolate.) Remove measuring cup from saucepan. Let chocolate cool slightly.

2. Fill plastic bag about half full with melted chocolate. Seal bag securely. Cut small corner off bottom of plastic bag.

3. Position sealed end of bag in your writing hand. Position fingers near opening of bag; place other hand under bag to guide it. While gently squeezing bag, guide opening just above food to drizzle chocolate, in zigzag design, onto dessert, using even, steady flow. Stop squeezing and then lift bag at end of each design.

4. For chocolate shapes, prepare melted chocolate and fill plastic bag as directed in steps 1 and 2. Place sheet of waxed paper onto inverted baking sheet. While gently squeezing bag, guide opening just above waxed paper to pipe chocolate in steady flow, making variety of small shapes. Stop squeezing and then lift bag at end of each shape. Create flowers, hearts, lattice shapes or any lacy pattern.

5. Let stand in cool, dry place until chocolate is firm. (Do not chill in refrigerator.) When chocolate is firm, gently peel shapes off waxed paper using a small metal spatula. Store in cool, dry place until ready to use.

Clockwise from top left: Piped Cream Cheese, Chocolate Shapes, Strawberry Fan (page 14), Sugared Fruit (page 14), Scored Citrus Slice (page 13), Seasoned Butter Balls (page 20) and Caramel Roses (page 18).

23

Tomato/Orange Roses

Firm, ripe tomato or orange
Tiny fresh mint leaves (optional)

1. For tomato rose, cut very thin slice from bottom of tomato with paring knife; discard slice.

2. Starting at top of tomato, peel tomato with knife by cutting continuous narrow strip of peel in spiral fashion horizontally around entire tomato, using gentle sawing motion.

3. Place strip, either flesh or peel side up, on cutting board. Starting at end of strip where you started cutting, wrap strip around itself to form coil. Tuck end of strip underneath coil to secure. Place on food or plate and tuck two or three mint leaves at base of rose, if desired.

4. For orange rose, substitute orange for tomato. Starting at top of orange, cut continuous strip of peel, using vegetable peeler, in spiral fashion horizontally around entire orange, pressing firmly while peeling.

5. Starting at end of strip where you started cutting, wrap strip around itself to form coil. Continue wrapping peel tightly around coil, tapering bottom as much as possible. Insert one or two toothpicks horizontally into base of orange rose to secure.

6. Place orange rose on desired food or plate. Trim with mint leaves, if desired.

Bacon Curls

2 slices bacon, cut crosswise into thirds
SUPPLIES
6- to 8-inch metal skewers

Loosely roll up bacon pieces and thread about ½ inch apart on metal skewers. Place skewers, 1½ to 2 inches apart, on unheated rack of broiler pan. Position under preheated broiler so rack is about 5 inches from heat source. Broil 4 to 6 minutes or until bacon is crisp, turning every 2 minutes.* Cool. Carefully remove curls from skewers with fork. Drain on paper towels; cool completely.

Makes 6 bacon curls

Skewers will be hot. Be sure to wear oven mitts.

Helpful Hint

Many fruit and vegetable garnishes may be made up to one day ahead if they are wrapped in plastic wrap and refrigerated until ready to use. When working with apples or other fruits that brown when cut, generously brush the cut surfaces with lemon juice before wrapping and refrigerating.

Marzipan Cutouts/Fruits

1 can (8 ounces) almond paste
1 egg white*
3 cups powdered sugar
Paste or liquid food coloring
Additional powdered sugar (for cutouts)

Use only grade A clean, uncracked egg.

1. Combine almond paste and egg white in small bowl. Add 2 cups powdered sugar; mix well. Knead in remaining 1 cup sugar until smooth and pliable. Wrap tightly in plastic wrap; refrigerate until ready to use.

2. For marzipan cutouts, place desired amount of marzipan in small bowl. Tint by stirring in small amount of food coloring; mix well. Add additional food coloring, a little at a time, until marzipan is desired shade. Shape into a ball; flatten slightly. Place marzipan between two sheets of waxed paper dusted with powdered sugar. Roll to ⅛-inch thickness; discard top sheet of waxed paper. Cut marzipan into desired shapes with small cookie cutters, placing cutters as close together as possible. If desired, tint additional portions of marzipan different colors to make additional cutouts.

3. For marzipan fruits, divide desired amount of marzipan into small portions; place each portion in separate bowl. Tint by stirring enough food coloring into each portion to make desired shade.

4. To make lemons, roll small pieces of yellow marzipan into ovals. Roll ovals over rough surface of hand grater to make markings similar to lemon peel. Pinch both ends slightly to resemble lemons.

5. To make apples or oranges, roll small pieces of red or orange marzipan into balls. Press ends to flatten slightly for top and bottom. Make dent in top and bottom of each ball. To make leaves and stems, flatten small pieces of green marzipan to about ⅛-inch thickness. Cut out leaf shapes; mark each with leaf-vein pattern. Cut out stems from remaining green marzipan or use whole cloves. Attach stem and leaves to top of each apple or orange, pressing gently into fruit to secure.

25

COOKIES

Crayon Cookies

  1 **cup butter, softened**
  2 **teaspoons vanilla**
  ½ **cup powdered sugar**
2¼ **cups all-purpose flour**
  ¼ **teaspoon salt**
     Assorted paste food colorings
1½ **cups chocolate chips**
1½ **teaspoons shortening**

1. Preheat oven to 350°F. Grease cookie sheets.

2. Beat butter and vanilla in large bowl at high speed of electric mixer until fluffy. Add sugar; beat at medium speed until blended. Combine flour and salt in small bowl. Gradually add to butter mixture.

3. Divide dough into 10 equal sections. Reserve 1 section; cover and refrigerate remaining 9 sections. Combine reserved section and desired food coloring in small bowl; blend well.

4. Cut dough into 2 equal sections. Roll each section into 5-inch log. Pinch one end to resemble crayon tip. Place cookies 2 inches apart on prepared cookie sheets. Repeat with remaining 9 sections of dough and desired food colorings.

5. Bake 15 to 18 minutes or until edges are lightly browned. Cool completely on cookie sheets.

6. Combine chocolate chips and shortening in small microwavable bowl. Microwave at HIGH 1 to 1½ minutes, stirring after 1 minute, or until smooth. Fill resealable plastic bag about half full with melted chocolate. Seal bag securely. Cut small corner off bottom of bag. Decorate cookies with chocolate mixture to look like crayons. ***Makes 20 cookies***

Crayon Cookies

COOKIES

Peanut Butter and Jelly Sandwich Cookies

- **1 package (about 18 ounces) refrigerated sugar cookie dough**
- **1 tablespoon unsweetened cocoa powder**
- **All-purpose flour (optional)**
- **1¾ cups creamy peanut butter**
- **½ cup grape jam or jelly**

1. Remove dough from wrapper according to package directions. Reserve ¼ section of dough; cover and refrigerate remaining ¾ section of dough. Combine reserved dough and cocoa in small bowl; refrigerate.

2. Shape remaining ¾ section dough into 5½-inch log. Sprinkle with flour to minimize sticking, if necessary. Remove chocolate dough from refrigerator; roll on sheet of waxed paper to 9½×6½-inch rectangle. Place dough log in center of rectangle.

3. Bring waxed paper edges and chocolate dough up and together over log. Press gently on top and sides of dough so entire log is wrapped in chocolate dough. Flatten log slightly to form square. Wrap in waxed paper. Freeze 10 minutes.

4. Preheat oven to 350°F.

5. Remove waxed paper from dough. Cut into ¼-inch slices. Place slices 2 inches apart on ungreased cookie sheets. Reshape dough edges into square, if necessary. Press dough slightly to form indentation so dough resembles slice of bread.

6. Bake 8 to 11 minutes or until lightly browned. Remove from oven and straighten cookie edges with spatula. Cool 2 minutes on cookie sheets. Remove to wire racks; cool completely.

7. To make sandwich, spread about 1 tablespoon peanut butter on underside of 1 cookie. Spread about 1½ teaspoons jam over peanut butter; top with second cookie, pressing gently. Repeat with remaining cookies

Makes 11 sandwich cookies

Tip: *Cut each sandwich diagonally in half for a smaller cookie and fun look.*

Fun Fact

The seemingly endless variety of cookies can actually be divided into five basic types: bar, drop, refrigerator (slice and bake), rolled and shaped. These types are determined by the consistency of the dough and how it is formed into cookies.

Peanut Butter and Jelly Sandwich Cookies

COOKIES

Under the Sea

> **1 package (about 18 ounces) refrigerated sugar cookie dough**
> **Blue liquid or paste food coloring**
> **All-purpose flour (optional)**
> **Blue Royal Icing (recipe follows)**
> **Assorted small decors, gummy candies and hard candies**

1. Preheat oven to 350°F. Grease 12-inch pizza pan.

2. Remove dough from wrapper according to package directions. Combine dough and blue food coloring, a few drops at a time, in large bowl until desired color is achieved; blend until smooth. Sprinkle dough with flour to minimize sticking, if necessary.

3. Press dough into bottom of prepared pan, leaving about ¾-inch space between edge of dough and pan.

4. Bake 10 to 12 minutes or until set in center. Cool completely in pan on wire rack. Run spatula between cookie crust and pan after 10 to 15 minutes to loosen.

5. Spread Blue Royal Icing randomly over cookie to resemble texture of sea. Once icing is set, decorate with decors and candies as shown in photo.

Makes 10 to 12 wedges

Blue Royal Icing

> **1 egg white,* at room temperature**
> **2 to 2½ cups sifted powdered sugar**
> **½ teaspoon almond extract**
> **Blue liquid or paste food coloring**

*Use only grade A clean, uncracked egg.

1. Beat egg white in small bowl at high speed of electric mixer until foamy.

2. Gradually add 2 cups powdered sugar and almond extract. Beat at low speed until moistened. Increase mixer speed to high and beat until icing is stiff, adding additional powdered sugar if needed. Tint icing blue with food coloring, a few drops at a time, until desired color is achieved.

Under the Sea

COOKIES

Chocolate Chip Cordials

COOKIES
- 1 package **DUNCAN HINES® Chocolate Chip Cookie Mix**
- 1 **egg**
- ⅓ **cup canola oil**
- 3 **tablespoons water**
- 1⅓ **cup chopped pecans**
- ⅓ **cup chopped red candied cherries**
- ⅓ **cup flaked coconut**
- **Pecan or cherry halves for garnish**

CHOCOLATE GLAZE
- 1½ **squares (1½ ounces) semi-sweet chocolate**
- 3 **tablespoons butter or margarine**

1. Preheat oven to 375°F. Place 1¾-inch paper liners in 28 mini muffin cups.

2. For cookies, combine cookie mix, egg, oil and water in large bowl. Stir until thoroughly blended. Stir in chopped pecans, chopped cherries and coconut. Fill cups with cookie dough. Top with pecan or cherry halves. Bake at 375°F for 13 to 15 minutes or until light golden brown. Cool completely.

3. For chocolate glaze, melt chocolate and butter in small bowl over hot water. Stir until smooth. Drizzle over cordials. Refrigerate until chocolate is firm. Store in airtight container. *Makes 28 cordials*

Cookie Pops

- 1 **package (20 ounces) refrigerated sugar cookie dough**
- **All-purpose flour (optional)**
- 20 **(4-inch) lollipop sticks**
- **Assorted colored sugars, frostings, glazes and gels**

1. Preheat oven to 350°F. Grease cookie sheets.

2. Remove dough from wrapper according to package directions. Sprinkle with flour to minimize sticking, if necessary.

3. Cut dough in half. Reserve 1 half; refrigerate remaining dough. Roll reserved dough to ⅛-inch thickness. Cut out cookies using 3½-inch cookie cutters.

4. Place lollipop sticks on cookies so that tips of sticks are imbedded in cookies. Carefully turn cookies so sticks are in back; place on prepared cookie sheets. Repeat with remaining dough.

5. Bake 7 to 11 minutes or until edges are lightly browned. Cool cookies on cookie sheets 2 minutes. Remove cookies to wire racks; cool completely.

6. Decorate with colored sugars, frostings, glazes and gels as desired.

Makes 20 cookies

Swiss Mocha Treats

2 ounces imported Swiss bittersweet chocolate candy bar, broken
½ cup plus 2 tablespoons butter, softened and divided
1 tablespoon instant espresso powder
1 teaspoon vanilla
1¾ cups all-purpose flour
½ teaspoon baking soda
½ teaspoon salt
¾ cup sugar
1 large egg
3 ounces imported Swiss white chocolate candy bar, broken

Melt bittersweet chocolate and 2 tablespoons butter in small, heavy saucepan over low heat, stirring often. Add espresso powder; stir until dissolved. Remove mixture from heat; stir in vanilla. Let cool to room temperature.

Place flour, baking soda and salt in medium bowl; stir to combine. Beat ½ cup butter and sugar in large bowl with electric mixer at medium speed until light and fluffy. Beat in bittersweet chocolate mixture and egg. Gradually add flour mixture. Beat at low speed until well blended. Cover; refrigerate 30 minutes or until firm.

Preheat oven to 375°F. Roll tablespoonfuls of dough into 1-inch balls. Place balls 3 inches apart on ungreased cookie sheets. Flatten each ball into ½-inch-thick round with fork dipped in sugar. Bake 9 to 10 minutes or until set (do not overbake or cookies will become dry). Immediately remove cookies to wire racks; cool completely.

Place white chocolate in small resealable plastic freezer bag; seal bag. Microwave at MEDIUM (50% power) 1 minute. Turn bag over; microwave at MEDIUM 1 minute or until melted. Knead bag until chocolate is smooth. Cut off very tiny corner of bag; pipe or drizzle white chocolate decoratively onto cooled cookies. Let stand at room temperature 30 minutes or until set. Store tightly covered at room temperature or freeze up to 3 months.

Makes about 4 dozen cookies

Helpful Hint

Before drizzling cookies with chocolate or icing, or dusting with powdered sugar, place waxed paper under the wire rack to make cleaning up easier.

33

COOKIES

Chocolate-Dipped Orange Logs

3¼ cups all-purpose flour
⅓ teaspoon salt
1 cup butter, softened
1 cup sugar
2 eggs
1½ teaspoons grated orange peel
1 teaspoon vanilla
1 package (12 ounces) semisweet chocolate chips
1½ cups pecan pieces, finely chopped

Combine flour and salt in medium bowl. Beat butter in large bowl with electric mixer at medium speed until smooth. Gradually beat in sugar; increase speed to high and beat until light and fluffy. Beat in eggs, 1 at a time, blending well after each addition. Beat in orange peel and vanilla until blended. Gradually stir in flour mixture until blended. (Dough will be crumbly.)

Gather dough together and press gently to form ball. Flatten into disk; wrap in plastic wrap and refrigerate 2 hours or until firm. (Dough can be prepared one day in advance and refrigerated overnight.)

Preheat oven to 350°F. Shape dough into 1-inch balls. Roll balls on flat surface to form 3-inch logs about ½ inch thick. Place logs 1 inch apart on ungreased cookie sheets.

Bake 17 minutes or until bottoms of cookies are golden brown. (Cookies will feel soft and look white on top; they will become crisp when cool.) Transfer to wire racks to cool completely.

Melt chocolate chips in heavy saucepan over low heat. Place chopped pecans on sheet of waxed paper. Dip one end of each cookie in chocolate, shaking off excess. Roll chocolate-covered ends with pecans. Place on waxed paper-lined cookie sheets and let stand until chocolate is set, or refrigerate about 5 minutes to set chocolate. Store in airtight container.   *Makes about 36 cookies*

Chocolate-Dipped Orange Logs

COOKIES

Moons and Stars

> 1 cup butter, softened
> 1 cup sugar
> 1 egg
> 2 teaspoons lemon peel
> ½ teaspoon almond extract
> 3 cups all-purpose flour
> ½ cup ground almonds
>   All-purpose flour (optional)
>   Assorted colored icings, hard candies and colored sprinkles

1. Preheat oven to 350°F. Grease cookie sheets.

2. Beat butter, sugar, egg, lemon peel and almond extract in large bowl at medium speed of electric mixer until light and fluffy.

3. Combine flour and almonds in medium bowl. Add flour mixture to butter mixture; stir just until combined.

4. Roll dough on lightly floured surface to ⅛- to ¼-inch thickness. Cut out cookies using moon and star cookie cutters. Place cookies 2 inches apart on prepared cookie sheets.

5. Bake 7 to 9 minutes or until set but not browned. Cool on cookie sheets 2 minutes. Remove to wire rack; cool completely. Decorate cookies with icings, candies and sprinkles as shown in photo.   ***Makes about 4 dozen cookies***

Thumbprints

> 1 package (20 ounces) refrigerated sugar or chocolate cookie dough
>   All-purpose flour (optional)
> ¾ cup plus 1 tablespoon fruit preserves, any flavor

1. Grease cookie sheets. Remove dough from wrapper according to package directions. Sprinkle with flour to minimize sticking, if necessary.

2. Cut dough into 26 (1-inch) slices. Roll slices into balls, sprinkling with additional flour, if necessary. Place balls 2 inches apart on prepared cookie sheets. Press deep indention in center of each ball with thumb. Freeze dough 20 minutes.

3. Preheat oven to 350°F. Bake cookies 12 to 13 minutes or until edges are light golden brown (cookies will have started to puff up and loose their shape). Quickly press down indentation using tip of teaspoon.

4. Return to oven 2 to 3 minutes or until cookies are golden brown and set. Cool cookies completely on cookie sheets. Fill each indentation with about 1½ teaspoons preserves.   ***Makes 26 cookies***

Helpful Hint

For cutout cookies, chill cookie dough before rolling for easier handling. Remove only enough dough from the refrigerator to work with at one time.

Moons and Stars

Minty Shortbread Squares

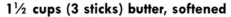

1½ **cups (3 sticks) butter, softened**
1½ **cups powdered sugar**
2 **teaspoons mint extract, divided**
3 **cups all-purpose flour**
½ **cup unsweetened cocoa powder**
1¾ **cups "M&M's"® Chocolate Mini Baking Bits, divided**
1 **16-ounce container prepared white frosting**
Several drops green food coloring

Preheat oven to 325°F. Lightly grease 15×10×1-inch baking pan; set aside. In large bowl cream butter and sugar until light and fluffy; add 1 teaspoon mint extract. In medium bowl combine flour and cocoa powder; blend into creamed mixture. Stir in 1 cup "M&M's"® Chocolate Mini Baking Bits. Dough will be stiff. Press dough into prepared baking pan with lightly floured fingers. Bake 16 to 18 minutes. Cool completely. Combine frosting, remaining 1 teaspoon mint extract and green food coloring. Spread frosting over shortbread; sprinkle with remaining ¾ cup "M&M's"® Chocolate Mini Baking Bits. Cut into squares. Store in tightly covered container. *Makes 36 squares*

Variation: Use 1 (19- to 21-ounce) package fudge brownie mix, prepared according to package directions for chewy brownies, adding 1 teaspoon mint extract to liquid ingredients. Stir in 1 cup "M&M's"® Chocolate Mini Baking Bits. Spread dough in lightly greased 13×9×2-inch baking pan. Bake in preheated oven according to package directions. Cool completely. Prepare frosting and decorate as directed above. Store in tightly covered container. Makes 24 squares.

Butter Pretzel Cookies

1 **recipe Butter Cookie Dough (page 130)**
White, rainbow or colored rock or coarse sugar

1. Prepare Butter Cookie Dough. Cover; refrigerate about 4 hours or until firm.

2. Preheat oven to 350°F. Grease cookie sheets.

3. Divide dough into 4 equal sections. Reserve 1 section; refrigerate remaining 3 sections. Divide reserved dough into 4 equal pieces. Roll each dough piece on lightly floured surface to 12-inch rope; sprinkle with rock or coarse sugar.

4. Transfer 1 rope at a time to prepared cookie sheets. Form each rope into pretzel shape. Repeat steps with remaining dough pieces.

5. Bake 14 to 18 minutes or until edges begin to brown. Cool cookies on cookie sheets 1 minute. Remove to wire racks; cool completely. *Makes 16 cookies*

Minty Shortbread Squares

COOKIES

Danish Raspberry Ribbons

1 **cup butter, softened**
½ **cup granulated sugar**
1 **large egg**
2 **tablespoons milk**
2 **tablespoons vanilla**
¼ **teaspoon almond extract**
2⅔ **cups all-purpose flour**
6 **tablespoons seedless raspberry jam**
  Glaze (recipe follows)

1. Beat butter and sugar in large bowl with electric mixer at medium speed until light and fluffy, scraping down side of bowl once. Beat in egg, milk, vanilla and almond extract until well blended, scraping down side of bowl once.

2. Gradually add 1½ cups flour. Beat at low speed until well blended, scraping down side of bowl occasionally. Stir in enough remaining flour with spoon to form stiff dough. Form dough into disc; wrap in plastic wrap and refrigerate until firm, at least 30 minutes or overnight.

3. Preheat oven to 375°F. Cut dough into 6 equal pieces. Rewrap 3 dough pieces and return to refrigerator. With floured hands, shape each piece of dough into 12-inch-long, ¾-inch-thick rope.

4. Place ropes 2 inches apart on ungreased cookie sheets. Make lengthwise ¼-inch-deep groove down center of each rope with handle of wooden spoon or finger. (Ropes will flatten to ½-inch-thick strips.)

5. Bake 12 minutes. Remove from oven; spoon 1 tablespoon jam into each groove. Return to oven; bake 5 to 7 minutes longer or until strips are light golden brown. Cool strips 15 minutes on cookie sheet.

6. Prepare Glaze. Drizzle strips with Glaze; let stand 5 minutes to set. Cut cookie strips at 45° angle into 1-inch slices. Place cookies on wire racks; cool completely. Repeat with remaining dough.

7. Store tightly covered between sheets of waxed paper at room temperature.

Makes about 5½ dozen cookies

Glaze

Combine ½ cup powdered sugar, 1 tablespoon milk and 1 teaspoon vanilla in small bowl. Stir until smooth.

Danish Raspberry Ribbons

COOKIES

Tasty Tidbit

For extra flavor and crunch, roll these cookies in chopped toasted nuts after dipping in melted chocolate.

Double-Dipped Chocolate Peanut Butter Cookies

1¼ **cups all-purpose flour**
½ **teaspoon baking powder**
½ **teaspoon baking soda**
½ **teaspoon salt**
½ **cup butter, softened**
½ **cup granulated sugar**
½ **cup packed light brown sugar**
½ **cup creamy or chunky peanut butter**
1 **large egg**
1 **teaspoon vanilla**
1½ **cups semisweet chocolate chips**
1½ **cups milk chocolate chips**
3 **teaspoons shortening, divided**

1. Preheat oven to 350°F. Place flour, baking powder, baking soda and salt in small bowl; stir to combine.

2. Beat butter, granulated sugar and brown sugar in large bowl with electric mixer at medium speed until light and fluffy, scraping down side of bowl once. Beat in peanut butter, egg and vanilla, scraping down side of bowl once. Gradually stir in flour mixture, blending well.

3. Roll heaping tablespoonfuls of dough into 1½-inch balls. Place balls 2 inches apart on ungreased cookie sheets. (If dough is too soft to roll into balls, refrigerate 30 minutes.) Dip table fork into granulated sugar; press criss-cross fashion onto each ball, flattening to ½-inch thickness. Bake 12 minutes or until set. Let cookies stand on cookie sheets 2 minutes. Remove cookies to wire rack; cool completely.

4. Melt semisweet chocolate chips and 1½ teaspoons shortening in top of double boiler over hot, not boiling, water. Dip one end of each cookie one third the way up; place on waxed paper. Let stand until chocolate is set, about 30 minutes.

5. Melt milk chocolate chips with 1½ teaspoons shortening in top of double boiler over hot, not boiling, water. Dip opposite end of each cookie one third the way up; place on waxed paper. Let stand until chocolate is set, about 30 minutes.

6. Store cookies between sheets of waxed paper at cool room temperature or freeze up to 3 months. *Makes about 2 dozen (3-inch) cookie*

Rainbows

1 recipe Christmas Ornament Cookie Dough (page 131)
Red, green, yellow and blue paste food colors
White frosting and edible gold glitter dust

1. Prepare Christmas Ornament Cookie Dough. Divide dough into 10 equal sections. Combine 4 sections dough and red food coloring in large bowl; blend until smooth.

2. Combine 3 sections dough and green food coloring in medium bowl; blend until smooth.

3. Combine 2 sections dough and yellow food coloring in another medium bowl; blend until smooth.

4. Combine remaining dough and blue food coloring in small bowl; blend until smooth. Wrap each section of dough in plastic wrap. Refrigerate 30 minutes.

5. Shape blue dough into 8-inch log. Shape yellow dough into 8×3-inch rectangle; place on waxed paper. Place blue log in center of yellow rectangle. Fold yellow edges up and around blue log, pinching to seal. Roll gently to form smooth log.

6. Roll green dough into 8×5-inch rectangle on waxed paper. Place yellow log in center of green rectangle. Fold green edges up and around yellow log. Pinch to seal. Roll gently to form smooth log.

7. Roll red dough into 8×7-inch rectangle. Place green log in center of red rectangle. Fold red edges up and around green log. Pinch to seal. Roll gently to form smooth log. Wrap in plastic wrap. Refrigerate 1 hour.

8. Preheat oven to 350°F. Grease cookie sheets. Cut log in half lengthwise. Cut each half into ¼-inch-thick slices. Place slices 1 inch apart on prepared cookie sheets. Bake 8 to 12 minutes. (Do not brown.) Cool on cookie sheets 1 minute. Remove to wire racks; cool completely.

9. Pipe small amount of frosting on bottom corner of 1 side of each cookie and sprinkle with glitter dust. Let stand 1 hour or until frosting sets.

Makes about 5 dozen cookies

COOKIES

Cookie Cups

1 package (20 ounces) refrigerated sugar cookie dough
All-purpose flour (optional)
Prepared pudding, nondairy whipped topping, maraschino
cherries, jelly beans, assorted sprinkles and small candies

1. Grease 12 (2¾-inch) muffin cups. Remove dough from wrapper according to package directions. Sprinkle dough with flour to minimize sticking, if necessary.

2. Cut dough into 12 equal pieces; roll into balls. Place 1 ball in bottom of each muffin cup. Press dough halfway up sides of muffin cup, making indentation in center of dough. Freeze muffin cups 15 minutes. Preheat oven to 350°F.

3. Bake 15 to 17 minutes or until golden brown. Cookies will be puffy. Remove from oven; gently press indentation with teaspoon. Return to oven 1 to 2 minutes. Cool cookies in muffin cups 5 minutes. Remove to wire racks; cool completely.

4. Fill each cookie cup with desired fillings. Decorate as desired.

Makes 12 cookie cups

Oatmeal Candied Chippers

  ¾ **cup butter, softened**
  ¾ **cup granulated sugar**
  ¾ **cup packed light brown sugar**
  3 **tablespoons milk**
  1 **egg**
  2 **teaspoons vanilla**
  ¾ **cup all-purpose flour**
  ¾ **teaspoon salt**
  ½ **teaspoon baking soda**
  3 **cups uncooked rolled oats**
1⅓ **cups (10-ounce package) candy-coated chocolate pieces**

Preheat oven to 375°F. Grease cookie sheets; set aside. Beat butter and sugars in large bowl until light and fluffy. Add milk, egg and vanilla; beat well. Add flour, salt and baking soda. Beat until well combined. Stir in oats and chocolate pieces.

Drop by rounded tablespoonfuls 2 inches apart on prepared cookie sheets. Bake 10 to 12 minutes until edges are golden brown. Let cookies stand 2 minutes on cookie sheets. Remove cookies to wire racks; cool completely.

Makes about 4 dozen cookies

Cookie Cups

COOKIES

Fun Fact

The word cookie comes from the Dutch word koekje meaning "little cake." The Dutch brought these little cakes to their first settlements in America, and they have been popular ever since. With so many flavors, shapes and sizes to choose from, cookies have definitely earned their place as America's favorite snack food.

Cookie Bowl and Cookie Fruit

- 1 cup butter, softened
- 1½ cups sugar
- 2 whole eggs
- 2 teaspoons grated orange peel
- 2 teaspoons vanilla
- 5 cups all-purpose flour
- 1 teaspoon baking powder
- ½ teaspoon salt
- 1 cup sour cream
- 4 egg yolks, divided
- 4 teaspoons water, divided
- Red, yellow, blue and green liquid food colors

SUPPLIES
Small, clean paintbrushes or pastry brushes

1. Beat butter and sugar in large bowl at high speed of electric mixer until light and fluffy. Add whole eggs, orange peel and vanilla; mix until well blended.

2. Combine flour, baking powder and salt in another large bowl. Add half of flour mixture to butter mixture; mix at low speed until well blended. Add sour cream; mix well. Add remaining flour mixture; mix well.

3. Divide dough into 4 equal sections. Cover; refrigerate several hours or overnight.

4. Place 1 egg yolk in each of 4 separate bowls. Add 1 teaspoon water and food color to each; beat lightly. Set aside.

5. Preheat oven to 375°F. Roll 1 section of dough on well-floured surface to 12-inch circle. Carefully transfer to inverted 1½-quart ovenproof bowl. Press overlapping portions of dough together; trim edges. Paint sides of bowl as desired using paintbrushes and egg yolk paint.

6. Place bowl on wire rack and then on cookie sheet. Bake 20 to 25 minutes or until lightly browned. Cool completely on bowl.

7. Roll remaining dough on well-floured surface to ⅛-inch thickness. Cut with fruit shaped cookie cutters. Place 2 inches apart on ungreased cookie sheets. Paint as desired with egg yolk paint.

8. Bake 10 to 12 minutes or until edges are lightly browned. Remove to wire racks; cool completely.

Makes 1 bowl and 4 dozen cookies

Cookie Bowl and Cookie Fruit

47

COOKIES

Peanut Butter Kisses

1¼ **cups firmly packed light brown sugar**
¾ **cup creamy peanut butter**
½ **cup CRISCO® all-vegetable shortening**
3 **tablespoons milk**
1 **tablespoon vanilla**
1 **egg**
1¾ **cups all-purpose flour**
¾ **teaspoon baking soda**
¾ **teaspoon salt**
 Granulated sugar
48 **chocolate kisses, unwrapped**

1. Heat oven to 375°F. Place sheets of foil on countertop for cooling cookies.

2. Combine brown sugar, peanut butter, ½ cup shortening, milk and vanilla in large bowl. Beat at medium speed of electric mixer until well blended. Add egg. Beat just until blended.

3. Combine flour, baking soda and salt. Add to shortening mixture; beat at low speed just until blended.

4. Form dough into 1-inch balls. Roll in granulated sugar. Place 2 inches apart on ungreased baking sheets.

5. Bake one baking sheet at a time at 375°F for 6 minutes. Press chocolate kiss into center of each cookie. Return to oven. Bake 3 minutes. *Do not overbake.* Cool 2 minutes on baking sheets. Remove cookies to foil to cool completely.

Makes about 3 dozen cookies

Fruity Cookie Rings and Twists

1 **package (20 ounces) refrigerated sugar cookie dough**
3 **cups fruit-flavored cereal, crushed and divided**

1. Remove dough from wrapper according to package directions.

2. Combine dough and ½ cup cereal in large bowl. Divide dough into 32 balls. Refrigerate 1 hour.

3. Preheat oven to 375°F. Roll dough balls into 6- to 8-inch-long ropes. Roll ropes in remaining cereal to coat; shape into rings or fold in half and twist.

4. Place cookies 2 inches apart on ungreased cookie sheets.

5. Bake 10 to 11 minutes or until lightly browned. Remove to wire racks; cool completely.

Makes 32 cookies

Peanut Butter Kisses

CAKES

Black Forest Cake

- 2 cups plus 2 tablespoons all-purpose flour
- 2 cups granulated sugar
- ¾ cup cocoa
- 1½ teaspoons baking powder
- ¾ teaspoon baking soda
- ¾ teaspoon salt
- 3 eggs
- 1 cup milk
- ½ cup vegetable oil
- 1 tablespoon vanilla
  - Cherry Topping (page 52)
  - Frosting (page 52)

SUPPLIES
Decorating bag and large star tip

1. Preheat oven to 350°F. Grease and flour two (9-inch) round cake pans. Line bottoms with waxed paper; set aside. Mix dry ingredients in large bowl. Add eggs, milk, oil and vanilla; beat until well blended. Pour evenly into prepared pans.

2. Bake 35 minutes or until wooden pick inserted in centers comes out clean. Cool layers in pans on wire racks 10 minutes. Remove layers to racks; cool. Prepare Cherry Topping; cool. Prepare Frosting.

3. With long serrated knife, split each cake layer horizontally in half. Crumble one split layer; set aside.

4. Reserve 1½ cups Frosting. To assemble, place one cake layer on cake plate. Spread with 1 cup Frosting; top with ¾ cup Cherry Topping. Top with cake layer; repeat layers of Frosting and Cherry Topping. Top with cake layer.

5. Frost side of cake with remaining Frosting. Pat reserved crumbs onto side. Using star tip and reserved Frosting, pipe on top and bottom of cake. Spoon remaining Cherry Topping on top of cake. *Makes one 3-layer cake*

continued on page 52

Black Forest Cake

CAKES

Black Forest Cake, continued from page 50

Cherry Topping

> **2 (20-ounce) cans tart pitted cherries, undrained**
> **1 cup granulated sugar**
> **¼ cup cornstarch**
> **1 teaspoon vanilla**

Drain cherries, reserving ½ cup juice. Combine reserved juice, cherries, sugar and cornstarch in 2-quart saucepan. Cook over low heat until thickened, stirring constantly. Stir in 1 teaspoon vanilla. Cool; set aside.

Frosting

Beat 3 cups cold whipping cream and ⅓ cup powdered sugar in chilled deep medium bowl at high speed with electric mixer until stiff peaks form.

Philly 3-Step® Raspberry Swirl Cheesecake

> **2 packages (8 ounces each) PHILADELPHIA® Cream Cheese, softened**
> **½ cup sugar**
> **½ teaspoon vanilla**
> **2 eggs**
> **1 ready-to-use graham cracker crust (6 ounces or 9-inch)**
> **3 tablespoons red raspberries preserves**

1. MIX cream cheese, sugar and vanilla at medium speed with electric mixer until well blended. Add eggs; mix until blended.

2. POUR into crust. Dot top of cheesecake with preserves. Cut through batter with knife several times for marble effect.

3. BAKE at 350°F for 40 minutes or until center is almost set. Cool. Refrigerate 3 hours or overnight. Garnish with COOL WHIP Whipped Topping and raspberries.   *Makes 8 servings*

Philly 3-Step® Peaches and Cream Cheesecake: *Substitute ¼ cup peach preserves for red raspberry preserves.*

Prep Time: 10 minutes
Baking Time: 40 minutes

Philly 3-Step® Raspberry Swirl Cheesecake

CAKES

Tasty Tidbit

Add pizzazz to any cake by mixing in ¾ cup chocolate chips or nuts to the batter before baking. Or for a burst of color when the cake is cut, mix in ¼ cup colored sprinkles.

Let's Play Ball!

4 cups cake batter*
1 recipe Jam Glaze (recipe follows), if desired
1½ cups Chocolate Buttercream Frosting (page 136)
2 cups Buttercream Frosting (page 136)
1 black licorice whip
Black and red paste food coloring

SUPPLIES
1 (10-inch) round cake board, covered, or large plate
Decorating bags, small and medium writing tips

A 2-layer cake recipe or mix will yield about 4 cups cake batter.

1. Preheat oven to 350°F. Grease and flour 9-inch round cake pan and 1-quart ovenproof bowl. Pour 2½ cups cake batter into prepared round pan and remaining batter into prepared bowl. Bake cake in pan 35 minutes or until wooden pick inserted into center comes out clean. Bake cake in bowl 40 minutes or until wooden pick inserted into center comes out clean. Let cakes cool in pan or bowl 10 minutes. Loosen edge; invert onto wire rack and cool completely.

2. Prepare Jam Glaze. Trim top of round cake and flat side of bowl cake. Cut round cake as shown in photo; place on prepared cake board. Brush cake lightly with Jam Glaze. Let dry 1 hour.

3. Frost glove with Chocolate Buttercream Frosting. Reserve ½ cup Buttercream Frosting for white frosting. Tint ½ cup frosting black and ½ cup red. Using medium writing tip and black frosting, pipe around edge of glove, forming fingers of glove as shown in photo. Cut licorice whip into four 2-inch pieces. Crisscross across space between thumb and fingers of glove.

4. Place bowl cake on glove flat-side down. Frost with white frosting. Using small writing tip and red frosting, pipe seams on baseball as shown.

Makes 16 to 18 servings

Jam Glaze

Bring 1 cup apricot or seedless raspberry jam and 1 tablespoon water to a boil in small saucepan. Remove from heat. Cool before using. Spread over cake and let stand about 1 hour before frosting.

Note: *Use apricot jam if the cake is being covered by a light frosting. The raspberry jam is particularly good with chocolate cake and frosting.*

Let's Play Ball!

CAKES

Chocolate Streusel Cake

STREUSEL
- 1 package **DUNCAN HINES® Moist Deluxe® Devil's Food Cake Mix, divided**
- 1 **cup finely chopped pecans**
- 2 **tablespoons brown sugar**
- 2 **teaspoons ground cinnamon**

CAKE
- 3 **eggs**
- 1⅓ **cups water**
- ½ **cup vegetable oil**

TOPPING
- 1 **container (8 ounces) frozen whipped topping, thawed**
- 3 **tablespoons sifted unsweetened cocoa**
  Chopped pecans, for garnish (optional)
  Chocolate curls, for garnish (optional)

1. Preheat oven to 350°F. Grease and flour 10-inch Bundt pan.

2. For streusel, combine 2 tablespoons cake mix, 1 cup pecans, brown sugar and cinnamon. Set aside.

3. For cake, combine remaining cake mix, eggs, water and oil in large bowl. Beat at medium speed with electric mixer for 2 minutes. Pour two-thirds of batter into pan. Sprinkle with reserved streusel. Pour remaining batter evenly over streusel. Bake at 350°F for 55 to 60 minutes or until toothpick inserted in center comes out clean. Cool in pan 25 minutes. Invert onto serving plate. Cool completely.

4. For topping, place whipped topping in medium bowl. Fold in cocoa until blended. Spread on cooled cake. Garnish with chopped pecans and chocolate curls, if desired. Refrigerate until ready to serve.   *Makes 12 to 16 servings*

Tip: For chocolate curls, warm chocolate in microwave oven at HIGH (100% power) for 5 to 10 seconds. Make chocolate curls by holding a sharp vegetable peeler against flat side of chocolate block and bringing blade toward you. Apply firm pressure for thicker, more open curls or light pressure for tighter curls.

Chocolate Streusel Cake

CAKES

1 (8-inch) square cake
1 recipe Creamy White Frosting (page 137)
 Yellow and blue paste food coloring
1 to 2 tablespoons milk
1 (3-inch) peppermint candy stick
 Assorted tiny multi-colored candies and sprinkles

SUPPLIES
 1 (19×13-inch) cake board, cut to fit cake if desired, covered

1. If cake top is rounded, trim horizontally with long serrated knife. Trim sides of cake. Cut cake as shown in diagram 1 with serrated knife, using ruler as guide. Freeze pieces 30 to 45 minutes before frosting.

2. Tint 1½ cups Creamy White Frosting bright yellow and ¼ cup bright blue. Thin remaining frosting with milk, adding 1 teaspoon at a time, until frosting is a thin consistency.

3. Position pieces A, B and C on prepared cake board as shown in diagram 2, connecting with some of the yellow frosting. Frost sides and tops with thinned frosting to seal in crumbs; let set. Frost again with remaining yellow frosting.

4. For piece D, starting at point, carefully spread thinned frosting along the side, using long strokes in direction away from point until all sides are frosted; frost top; let set. Frost again with blue frosting. Position candy stick and piece D as shown in Diagram 2. Decorate with candies and sprinkles as desired.

Makes 8 to 10 servings

Helpful Hint

For cleaner cutting lines and fewer crumbs on cut-apart cakes, freeze the cake 30 to 45 minutes before cutting. Use the diagrams and photos as guides and follow the directions carefully. A ruler and toothpicks are helpful for marking designs and using as guides while cutting.

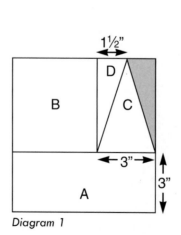

Diagram 1

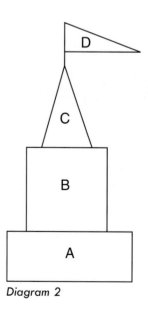

Diagram 2

A Little Country Pumpkin Cake

CAKE
- 2 cups boiling water
- ½ cup raisins
- 2 cups granulated sugar
- 1 cup melted **CRISCO®** all-vegetable shortening plus additional for greasing
- 1 can (16 ounces) solid-pack pumpkin (not pumpkin pie filling)
- 4 eggs
- 2 cups all-purpose flour
- 1 tablespoon ground cinnamon
- 2 teaspoons baking powder
- 1 teaspoon baking soda
- 1 teaspoon ground ginger
- ¾ teaspoon salt
- ¼ teaspoon ground cloves

FROSTING
- ¼ cup Butter Flavor* **CRISCO®** all-vegetable shortening
- 2 cups confectioners' sugar
- 3 tablespoons milk
- 1 teaspoon pure vanilla extract
- Chopped nuts

Butter Flavored Crisco® is artificially flavored.

1. Heat oven to 350°F. Grease 10-inch round cake pan. Flour lightly. Place cooling rack on counter top for cooling cake.

2. For cake, pour boiling water over raisins. Drain. Press to remove excess water.

3. Combine granulated sugar, 1 cup melted shortening, pumpkin and eggs in large bowl. Beat at medium-high speed of electric mixer 5 minutes. Combine flour, cinnamon, baking powder, baking soda, ginger, salt and cloves in medium bowl. Add to pumpkin mixture, 1 cup at a time, beating at low speed after each addition until blended. Stir in raisins with spoon. Pour into pan.

4. Bake for 55 to 60 minutes or until toothpick inserted in center comes out clean. DO NOT OVERBAKE. Remove cake to rack to cool. Cool 10 to 15 minutes before removing from pan. Place cake, top side up, on wire rack. Cool completely. Place cake on serving plate.

5. For frosting, melt ¼ cup shortening in small saucepan on low heat. Transfer to medium bowl. Add confectioners' sugar. Beat at low, then high speed until blended. Add milk and vanilla. Beat at high speed until smooth and frosting is of desired spreading consistency. Frost top and side of cake. Press nuts into side of cake and around outside top edge. *Makes one 10-inch round cake*

CAKES

Mocha Cake Roll with Creamy Chocolate Filling

- ¾ **cup granulated sugar**
- 2 **eggs**
- 3 **egg whites**
- ¼ **cup Prune Purée (recipe follows) or prepared prune butter**
- ¼ **cup coffee-flavored liqueur, divided**
- 2 **tablespoons instant coffee granules**
- 1 **cup all-purpose flour**
- ¼ **cup unsweetened cocoa powder, divided**
- ¼ **teaspoon salt**
  Powdered sugar
- 1½ **cups low-fat nondairy whipped topping**
  Additional low fat nondairy whipped topping and chocolate covered coffee beans for garnish

Preheat oven to 425°F. Coat 13×9×2-inch baking pan with vegetable cooking spray. Line pan with parchment or waxed paper; coat paper with vegetable cooking spray. In top of double boiler or bowl set over simmering water, combine granulated sugar, eggs and egg whites. Beat at high speed with portable electric mixer until tripled in volume, about 5 minutes. Beat in prune purée, 2 tablespoons liqueur and coffee granules until well blended; remove from heat. In medium bowl, combine flour, 2 tablespoons cocoa and salt. Sift flour mixture over egg mixture; gently fold in just until blended. Spread batter evenly in prepared pan. Bake in center of oven 10 minutes or until springy to the touch.

Meanwhile, lay cloth tea towel on work surface; dust evenly with powdered sugar. When cake is done, immediately loosen edges and invert onto towel. Gently peel off paper. Roll cake up in towel from narrow end. Place seam side down on wire rack; cool completely. Gently unroll cooled cake; brush with remaining 2 tablespoons liqueur. Combine whipped topping with remaining 2 tablespoons cocoa. Spread evenly over moistened cake. Reroll cake without towel. Place seam side down on serving plate. Dust with powdered sugar. Garnish with additional whipped topping and coffee beans. Cut into slices.

Makes 12 servings

Prune Purée

Combine 1⅓ cups (8 ounces) pitted prunes and 6 tablespoons hot water in container of food processor or blender. Pulse on and off until prunes are finely chopped and smooth. Store leftovers in a covered container in the refrigerator for up to two months. Makes 1 cup.

Favorite recipe from **California Prune Board**

Mocha Cake Roll with Creamy Chocolate Filling

CAKES

Football Cake

1 package DUNCAN HINES® Moist Deluxe® Devil's Food Cake Mix
DECORATOR FROSTING
  ¾ cup confectioners' sugar
  2 tablespoons shortening plus additional for greasing
  1 tablespoon cold water
  1 tablespoon non-dairy powdered creamer
  ¼ teaspoon vanilla extract
    Dash salt
  1 container DUNCAN HINES® Chocolate Frosting

1. Preheat oven to 350°F. Grease and flour 10-inch round cake pan. Prepare cake following package directions for basic recipe. Bake at 350°F 45 to 55 minutes or until toothpick inserted in center comes out clean.

2. For decorator frosting, combine confectioners' sugar, shortening, water, non-dairy powdered creamer, vanilla extract and salt in small bowl. Beat at medium speed with electric mixer 2 minutes. Add more confectioners' sugar to thicken or water to thin frosting as needed.

3. Cut cake and remove 2-inch slice from center. Arrange cake as shown. Spread chocolate frosting on sides and top of cake. Place basketweave tip in pastry bag. Fill with decorator frosting. Make white frosting laces on football.

Makes 12 to 16 servings

Tip: If a 10-inch round pan is not available, make 2 football cakes by following package directions for baking with two 9-inch round cake pans.

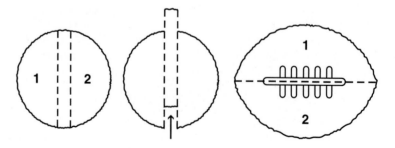

Football Cake

CAKES

Tasty Tidbit

Create great frosting flavors by adding ½ teaspoon flavored extract to vanilla frosting. For example, with chocolate cake, use almond or mint extract; with white, yellow or lemon cake, use orange or lemon extract.

Philly 3-Step® Mini Cheesecakes

> 2 **packages (8 ounces each) PHILADELPHIA® Cream Cheese, softened**
> ½ **cup sugar**
> ½ **teaspoon vanilla**
> 2 **eggs**
> 2 **packages (4 ounces each) ready-to-use single serve graham cracker crumb crusts (12 crusts)**
> **COOL WHIP® Whipped Topping, thawed**
> **Assorted tiny candies**

1. MIX cream cheese, sugar and vanilla with electric mixer on medium speed until well blended. Add eggs; mix until blended.

2. POUR into crusts placed on cookie sheet.

3. BAKE at 350°F for 20 minutes or until centers are almost set. Cool. Refrigerate 2 hours or overnight. Top with whipped topping and sprinkle with multicolored milk chocolate candies, candy corn, gummy bears or any tiny candies just before serving.   *Makes 12 servings*

Prep Time: 10 minutes
Baking Time: 20 minutes

I Think You're "Marbleous" Cupcakes

CAKE
> 1 **box (18.5 ounces) pudding-in-the-mix cake mix, any flavor**
> 1¼ **cups water**
> 3 **large eggs**
> ¼ **cup oil**
> 1 **can (16 ounces) vanilla frosting**
> 1 **tube (4.25 ounces) red decorating icing**

SUPPLIES
> **Decorating tips to fit tube of icing**

1. Preheat oven to 350°F. Grease or paper-line 24 (2½-inch) muffin cups.

2. Prepare cake mix according to package directions using water, eggs and oil. Spoon batter into prepared pans, filling each ⅔ full.

3. Bake 20 to 25 minutes or until toothpick inserted in center comes out clean. Cool in pans 20 minutes. Remove to wire rack and cool completely.

4. Spread 1½ to 2 tablespoons frosting over each cupcake. Fit writing tip onto icing. Squeeze 4 to 5 dots icing over each cupcake. Swirl toothpick through icing and frosting in continuous motion to make marbleized pattern or heart shapes.

Makes about 2 dozen

Philly 3-Step® Mini Cheesecakes

CAKES

Chocolate Midnight Cake

12 **ounces semisweet chocolate, coarsely chopped and divided**
 2 **squares (1 ounce each) unsweetened chocolate, coarsely chopped**
 1 **cup plus 1 tablespoon butter, divided**
 5 **eggs**
 ¼ **cup sugar**
 ⅓ **cup light corn syrup**
 ½ **teaspoon vanilla**
1⅓ **cups whipping cream, divided**
 ⅓ **cup powdered sugar**
 ¼ **cup fresh raspberries**
   Chocolate Curls (page 21)

SUPPLIES
Decorating bag and large star tip

1. Preheat oven to 325°F. Grease and flour 9-inch springform pan.

2. Melt 6 ounces semisweet chocolate, unsweetened chocolate and 1 cup butter over low heat in medium saucepan, stirring constantly; cool slightly. Beat eggs and sugar in large bowl. Add corn syrup and vanilla; beat well. Stir in chocolate mixture. Pour batter into prepared pan.

3. Bake 45 to 55 minutes or until wooden toothpick inserted in center of cake comes out clean. Cool completely in pan on wire rack. Remove side of pan.

4. Bring ⅔ cup cream and remaining 1 tablespoon butter to a simmer in small saucepan over low heat; remove from heat. Add remaining 6 ounces semisweet chocolate, stirring until completely melted. Pour into bowl; cover. Cool to room temperature or until mixture thickens but is still pourable.

5. Place cake on wire rack over waxed paper-lined baking sheet. Pour chocolate mixture over cake; spread to cover top and sides. Refrigerate until chilled, about 1 hour.

6. Beat remaining ⅔ cup cream and powdered sugar until soft peaks form. Using decorating bag and star tip, pipe along top edge of cake.

7. Place raspberries on cake in ring next to piped cream. Place chocolate curls in center of cake. Refrigerate until ready to serve. *Makes 10 servings*

Back-To-School Pencil Cake

1 package DUNCAN HINES® Moist Deluxe® Cake Mix (any flavor)
2 containers DUNCAN HINES® Creamy Homestyle Vanilla Frosting, divided
Red and yellow food coloring
Chocolate sprinkles

1. Preheat oven to 350°F. Grease and flour 13×9×2-inch pan.

2. Prepare, bake and cool cake following package directions for basic recipe.

3. For frosting, tint 1 cup Vanilla frosting pink with red food coloring. Tint remaining frosting with yellow food coloring.

4. To assemble, cut cooled cake as shown in Diagram 1 and arrange on large baking sheet or piece of sturdy cardboard as shown in Diagram 2. Spread pink frosting on cake for eraser at one end and for wood at other end. Spread yellow frosting over remaining cake. Decorate with chocolate sprinkles for pencil tip and eraser band.   *Makes 12 to 16 servings*

Tip: To make this cake even more special, reserve ¼ cup Vanilla frosting before tinting yellow. Place writing tip in decorating bag. Fill with frosting. Pipe name of child, teacher or school on pencil.

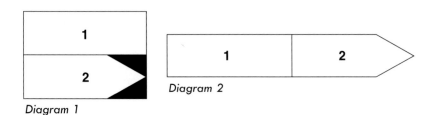

Diagram 1

Diagram 2

Paper-Doll Cake

CAKE

- 2 (8-inch) square cakes
- 1 recipe Fudge Frosting (page 138)
- 1 recipe Base Frosting (page 136)
  Powdered sugar
  Multi-colored flower-shaped cake decorations

SUPPLIES

- 1 (19×13-inch) cake board, cut to fit cake if desired, covered, or cake plate
- 1 (8-inch) waxed paper square

1. If cake tops are rounded, trim horizontally with long serrated knife. Trim sides of cakes.

2. Place one cake on prepared cake board. Frost top with about ½ cup Fudge Frosting. Place second cake on top. Frost top and sides with Base Frosting to seal in crumbs; let set. Frost again with remaining Fudge Frosting. Smooth frosting on top and sides.

3. To make paper-doll pattern, fold waxed paper in half. Fold in half again lengthwise. Draw paper-doll pattern about 4 inches tall with pencil. Cut out paper dolls with scissors, starting at folded edge. Unfold waxed paper. Position pattern across center of cake top and lightly press down edges.

4. Sift sugar generously around pattern, getting as little as possible on pattern. Brush sugar off pattern with fingertip. Carefully lift off pattern, holding pattern firmly by edges and pulling straight up. Use tip of toothpick to remove any sugar in pattern area.

5. Place cake decorations around edge of skirts or pants. Add decorations for bows on shoes or in hair.   *Makes 16 servings*

Paper-Doll Cake

CAKES

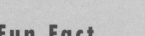

Apple Cider Cake

   1 **package (2-layer size) spice cake mix**
1¼ **cups apple cider**
   ⅓ **cup vegetable oil**
   3 **eggs**
      Apple Cider Filling (recipe follows)
      Apple Cider Frosting (recipe follows)
   2 **cups coarsely chopped walnuts**
      Marzipan Fruit (page 25)
      Marzipan Leaf Cutouts (page 25)

1. Preheat oven to 350°F. Grease and flour two 9-inch round baking pans.

2. Combine cake mix, apple cider, oil and eggs in medium bowl. Beat at low speed of electric mixer until blended; beat at medium speed 2 minutes. Pour batter evenly into prepared pans.

3. Bake 30 to 35 minutes until wooden toothpick inserted into centers comes out clean. Let cool in pans on wire racks 10 minutes. Remove to racks; cool.

4. Prepare Apple Cider Filling and Apple Cider Frosting. Place 1 cake layer on serving plate; top with Apple Cider Filling. Top with second cake layer; frost top and side of cake with Apple Cider Frosting. Press nuts onto side of cake. Arrange Marzipan Fruit and Marzipan Leaf Cutouts on top and around side of cake.

Makes 12 servings

Apple Cider Filling

   ⅓ **cup sugar**
   3 **tablespoons cornstarch**
   ⅔ **cup apple cider**
   ½ **cup apple butter**
   2 **tablespoons lemon juice**
   2 **tablespoons butter or margarine**

Combine sugar and cornstarch in small saucepan. Stir in cider and apple butter; cook over medium heat, stirring constantly, until thickened. Remove from heat; stir in lemon juice and butter. Cool completely.   *Makes about 1¼ cups*

Apple Cider Frosting

   ½ **cup butter or margarine, softened**
   ¼ **cup apple cider**
   4 **cups (about 1 pound) powdered sugar**

In medium bowl, beat butter and cider until creamy and well blended. Gradually beat in powdered sugar until smooth.   *Makes about 4 cups*

Apple Cider Cake

71

CAKES

Lucy the Ladybug

   4 cups cake batter*
1¾ cups Buttercream Frosting (page 136)
   2 tablespoons unsweetened cocoa powder
   2 teaspoons milk
   Assorted candies

SUPPLIES
   1 (10-inch) round cake board, covered, or large plate
   Decorating bag and medium writing tip

A 2-layer cake recipe or mix will yield about 4 cups cake batter.

1. Preheat oven to 350°F. Grease and flour 2-quart ovenproof bowl. Pour 4 cups cake batter into prepared bowl. Bake 1 hour and 15 minutes or until wooden pick inserted into center comes out clean. Cool 15 minutes in bowl. Loosen edge; invert on wire rack and cool completely.

2. Trim flat side of cake. Place on prepared cake board, flat-side down.

3. Tint 1 cup Buttercream Frosting red. Mix remaining ¾ cup frosting with unsweetened cocoa powder and milk.

4. Using wooden pick, mark semicircle about 3 inches from edge of cake for head as shown in photo. Frost remainder of cake with red frosting. Frost head with cocoa frosting, reserving small portion for piping.

5. Using writing tip and reserved cocoa frosting, pipe line down center from head to other edge. Pipe line between the head and body. Arrange assorted candies as shown.   *Makes 14 to 18 servings*

Lucy the Ladybug

CAKES

Pineapple-Coconut Party Cake

CAKE

- 2 cups granulated sugar
- 1 cup Butter Flavor* CRISCO® all-vegetable shortening plus additional for greasing
- 3 eggs
- 1 teaspoon pure vanilla extract
- 1 teaspoon coconut extract
- 3 cups sifted all-purpose flour
- 1 tablespoon baking powder
- 1 cup milk

TOPPING

- 1 can (20 ounces) crushed pineapple or pineapple tidbits in unsweetened juice
- 1 tablespoon cornstarch
- 1 cup firmly packed light brown sugar
- 1 cup shredded coconut
- 1 cup chopped pecans
- ½ teaspoon rum extract or ¼ cup rum
- ¼ teaspoon pure vanilla extract
- 12 to 16 maraschino cherries, drained

Butter Flavor Crisco® is artificially flavored.

1. Heat oven to 350°F. Grease 13×9×2-inch pan with shortening. Flour lightly.

2. For cake, combine granulated sugar and 1 cup shortening in large bowl. Beat at medium speed of electric mixer until light and fluffy. Add eggs, 1 at a time, beating well after each addition. Beat in 1 teaspoon vanilla and coconut extract until blended.

3. Combine flour and baking powder in medium bowl. Add to creamed mixture alternately with milk, beating at low speed after each addition until well blended. Beat at medium speed 2 minutes. Pour into pan. Spread evenly. (Batter will be very thick.)

4. Bake at 350°F for 35 to 45 minutes or until toothpick inserted in center comes out clean. (Cake will rise above top of pan and then fall slightly. Cake may be slightly lower in center.) Cool completely in pan on wire rack.

5. For topping, drain 2 tablespoons juice from pineapple. Combine juice and cornstarch in small bowl. Stir to dissolve.

6. Combine pineapple, remaining juice and brown sugar in medium saucepan. Bring to a boil. Stir in cornstarch mixture. Boil and stir 1 minute or until mixture is thickened and clear. Remove from heat. Stir in coconut, nuts, rum extract and ¼ teaspoon vanilla.

7. Use large fork or skewer to poke holes in top of cake. Pour topping over cake, spreading to edges. Arrange cherries on top of cake so that when cake is cut, each slice will have cherry in center. Refrigerate at least 30 minutes before serving. *Makes one 13×9×2-inch cake (12 to 16 servings)*

Note: Prepare cake and topping the day before serving, if desired.

Hot Fudge Sundae Cake

> **1 package DUNCAN HINES® Moist Deluxe® Dark Chocolate Fudge Cake Mix**
> **½ gallon brick vanilla ice cream**

FUDGE SAUCE
> **1 can (12 ounces) evaporated milk**
> **1¼ cups sugar**
> **4 squares (1 ounce each) unsweetened chocolate**
> **¼ cup butter or margarine**
> **1½ teaspoons vanilla extract**
> **¼ teaspoon salt**
> **Whipped cream and maraschino cherries, for garnish**

1. Preheat oven to 350°F. Grease and flour 13×9×2-inch pan. Prepare, bake and cool cake following package directions.

2. Remove cake from pan. Split cake in half horizontally. Place bottom layer back in pan. Cut ice cream into even slices and place evenly over bottom cake layer (use all the ice cream). Place remaining cake layer over ice cream. Cover and freeze.

3. For fudge sauce, combine evaporated milk and sugar in medium saucepan. Stir constantly on medium heat until mixture comes to a rolling boil. Boil and stir for 1 minute. Add unsweetened chocolate and stir until melted. Beat over medium heat until smooth. Remove from heat. Stir in butter, vanilla and salt.

4. Cut cake into serving squares. For each serving, place cake square on plate; spoon hot fudge sauce on top. Garnish with whipped cream and maraschino cherry. *Makes 12 to 16 servings*

Tip: Fudge sauce may be prepared ahead and refrigerated in tightly sealed jar. Reheat when ready to serve.

Lemon Chiffon Cloud Pie

CRUST

   1 (9-inch) Classic **CRISCO®** Crust (page 132)

FILLING

  ¾ **cup sugar**
   1 **envelope unflavored gelatin**
  ¼ **teaspoon salt**
   1 **cup water**
  ⅓ **cup strained, fresh lemon juice**
   2 **egg yolks, lightly beaten**
 1½ **teaspoons grated lemon peel**
 1½ **cups thawed frozen whipped topping**

GARNISH

  ½ **cup or more thawed frozen whipped topping**
    Thin strips of fresh lemon peel
    Fresh lemon slices and mint leaves

1. Prepare and bake 9-inch single crust as directed. Cool completely.

2. For filling, combine sugar, gelatin and salt in medium saucepan. Add water, lemon juice and egg yolks. Stir until well blended. Cook and stir on medium heat about 5 minutes or until gelatin is dissolved. Remove from heat. Stir in grated lemon peel. Transfer to medium bowl. Refrigerate until thickened.

3. Place bowl of filling in larger bowl containing ice and water. Beat at high speed of electric mixer 7 to 10 minutes or until double in volume. Fold in 1½ cups whipped topping. Spoon into cooled baked pie crust. Refrigerate at least 2 hours before serving.

4. For garnish, spoon ½ cup whipped topping into decorator bag fitted with large star tip. Pipe rosettes around edge of pie. Place lemon peel strips between rosettes. Pipe one large rosette in center of pie. Garnish as shown. Refrigerate leftovers.   *Makes one 9-inch pie (8 servings)*

Note: *Prepare Classic Crisco® Double Crust, if desired. Save half to make leaf cutouts to decorate edge of pie.*

Lemon Chiffon Cloud Pie

Fun Fact

Kiwifruit was originally cultivated in New Zealand and named for its national bird. Kiwifruit must be fully ripened for best flavor. Let firm kiwifruits ripen at room temperature until they yield to gentle palm pressure, then use right away or refrigerate.

Wisconsin Ricotta Tart with Kiwi and Raspberry Sauce

⅓ cup all-purpose flour
⅓ cup packed brown sugar
3 tablespoons butter
1 cup flaked coconut
½ cup chopped pecans or macadamia nuts
2 cups (16 ounces) Wisconsin Ricotta cheese
½ cup powdered sugar
1 teaspoon grated lime peel
1 teaspoon vanilla
1 package (10 ounces) frozen raspberries, thawed
1 kiwifruit

Preheat oven to 350°F. Combine flour and brown sugar; cut in butter until mixture resembles coarse crumbs. Stir in coconut and nuts. Press into 10-inch tart pan or pie plate. Bake crust 15 minutes. Remove from oven and cool.

Combine cheese, powdered sugar, lime peel and vanilla in food processor or blender; process until smooth. Spoon mixture into prepared crust. Refrigerate 1 hour. Before serving, place raspberries in food processor or blender; process until sauce forms. Cut kiwi into slices and arrange in circle on top of tart.* Drizzle tart with ½ of the raspberry sauce. Serve with remaining sauce.

Makes 8 to 10 servings

**Recipe can be prepared to this point and refrigerated until ready to serve.*

Favorite recipe from **Wisconsin Milk Marketing Board**

Wisconsin Ricotta Tart with Kiwi and Raspberry Sauce

Amaretto Coconut Cream Pie

- ¼ **cup flaked coconut**
- 1 **container (8 ounces) thawed nondairy whipped topping, divided**
- 1 **container (8 ounces) coconut cream-flavored or vanilla-flavored yogurt**
- ¼ **cup amaretto liqueur**
- 1 **package (4-serving size) instant coconut pudding and pie filling mix**
- 1 **prepared (9-inch) graham cracker pie crust**
- **Fresh strawberries and mint leaves (optional)**

Preheat oven to 350°F. To toast coconut, place coconut on baking sheet. Bake 4 to 5 minutes or until golden brown, stirring frequently. Cool completely.

Place 2 cups whipped topping, yogurt and amaretto in large bowl. Add pudding mix. Beat with wire whisk 1 to 2 minutes or until thickened.

Pour pudding mixture into crust; spread remaining whipped topping over filling. Sprinkle with toasted coconut. Garnish with fresh strawberries and mint leaves, if desired. Refrigerate. *Makes 8 servings*

Rice Pudding Tarts

- 1 **cup cooked rice**
- 1 **cup low-fat milk**
- ⅓ **cup sugar**
- ¼ **cup raisins**
- ⅛ **teaspoon salt**
- 2 **eggs, beaten**
- ¾ **cup heavy cream**
- ½ **teaspoon vanilla extract**
- ¼ **teaspoon almond extract**
- 6 **frozen tartlet pastry shells, partially baked and cooled**
- ⅛ **teaspoon ground nutmeg for garnish**
- **Fresh berries for garnish**
- **Fresh mint for garnish**

Combine rice, milk, sugar, raisins and salt in medium saucepan. Cook over medium-low heat 30 to 35 minutes or until thick and creamy, stirring frequently. Remove from heat; add ¼ rice mixture to eggs. Return egg mixture to saucepan; stir in cream and extracts. Spoon equally into pastry shells; sprinkle with nutmeg. Place tarts on baking sheet. Bake at 350°F 20 to 30 minutes or until pudding is set. Cool on wire rack 1 hour. Garnish with berries and mint. Serve at room temperature. Refrigerate remaining tarts. *Makes 6 servings*

Favorite recipe from **USA Rice Federation**

Amaretto Coconut Cream Pie

Mom's Lemon Meringue Pie

**Reduced-Fat Pie Pastry (page 133) or favorite pastry for
    9-inch pie**
2¼ **cups water**
½ **cup lemon juice**
10¾ **teaspoons EQUAL® FOR RECIPES or 36 packets EQUAL® sweetener
    or 1½ cups EQUAL® SPOONFUL™**
⅓ **cup plus 2 tablespoons cornstarch**
2 **eggs**
2 **egg whites**
1 **teaspoon finely grated lemon peel (optional)**
2 **tablespoons margarine**
1 **to 2 drops yellow food color (optional)**
3 **egg whites**
¼ **teaspoon cream of tartar**
3½ **teaspoons EQUAL® FOR RECIPES or 12 packets EQUAL®
    sweetener***

*Equal® Spoonful™ cannot be used in meringue recipes.

• Roll pastry on lightly floured surface into circle 1 inch larger than inverted 9-inch pie pan. Ease pastry into pan; trim and flute edge. Pierce bottom and side of pastry with fork. Bake in preheated 425°F oven until pastry is browned, 10 to 15 minutes. Cool on wire rack.

• Mix water, lemon juice, 10¾ teaspoons Equal® For Recipes or 36 packets Equal® sweetener or 1½ cups Equal® Spoonful™ and cornstarch in medium saucepan. Heat to boiling over medium-high heat, stirring constantly; boil and stir 1 minute. Beat eggs and 2 egg whites in small bowl; stir in about half of hot cornstarch mixture. Stir egg mixture back into remaining cornstarch mixture in saucepan; cook and stir over low heat 1 minute. Remove from heat; add lemon peel, if desired, and margarine, stirring until melted. Stir in food color, if desired. Pour mixture into baked pie shell.

• Beat 3 egg whites in medium bowl with electric mixer until foamy; add cream of tartar and beat to soft peaks. Gradually beat in 3½ teaspoons Equal® For Recipes or 12 packets Equal® sweetener, beating until stiff peaks form. Spread meringue over hot lemon filling, carefully sealing to edge of crust to prevent shrinking or weeping.

• Bake pie in preheated 425°F oven until meringue is browned, about 5 minutes. Cool completely on wire rack before cutting. *Makes 8 servings*

Cherry Cheese Pie

½ **recipe Rich Pie Pastry (page 133)**
1 **egg, lightly beaten**
   Granulated sugar
8 **ounces cream cheese, softened**
⅓ **cup firmly packed light brown sugar**
1 **egg**
1 **teaspoon almond extract**
1 **can (21 ounces) cherry pie filling**

1. Preheat oven to 375°F. Roll pastry on lightly floured surface to form 13-inch circle. Place in 9-inch pie plate. Trim and flute edges; set aside.

2. Reroll pastry scraps and cut into decorative shapes; place on baking sheet. Use tip of knife to decorate cutouts with designs, if desired. Brush cutouts with beaten egg; sprinkle with sugar. Bake cutouts 6 to 8 minutes or until golden brown.

3. Beat cream cheese and brown sugar until fluffy. Add whole egg and almond extract; blend well. Brush pie shell with remaining beaten egg. Pour cream cheese mixture into pie shell. Bake 18 to 20 minutes or until set. Cool completely on wire rack.

4. Spread cherry pie filling over cooled cheese layer. Decorate with pastry cutouts.

Makes 1 (9-inch) pie

Date-Nut Pumpkin Pie

CRUST

1 (9-inch) Classic **CRISCO®** Crust (page 132)

DATE-NUT LAYER

1 package (8 ounces) pitted whole dates, chopped

¾ cup water

⅓ cup firmly packed brown sugar

¼ cup butter or margarine

½ cup chopped walnuts

½ teaspoon cinnamon

FILLING

2 eggs

1½ cups mashed cooked pumpkin or canned solid-pack pumpkin (not pumpkin pie filling)

1 cup evaporated milk

½ cup granulated sugar

½ cup firmly packed brown sugar

½ teaspoon cinnamon

½ teaspoon ginger

½ teaspoon nutmeg

¼ teaspoon salt

⅛ teaspoon cloves

GARNISH

Sweetened whipped cream

1. Prepare 9-inch unbaked single crust as directed. Do not bake. Reserve dough scraps for cutouts, if desired.* Heat oven to 450°F.

2. For date-nut layer, combine dates and water in medium saucepan. Cook on medium heat until mixture comes to a boil and dates have softened. Add ⅓ cup brown sugar and butter. Stir to blend. Remove from heat. Stir in nuts and cinnamon. Cool while preparing filling.

3. For filling, beat eggs lightly in medium bowl. Add pumpkin, evaporated milk, granulated sugar, ½ cup brown sugar, spices and salt. Stir to blend.

4. Spoon date-nut mixture into unbaked pie crust. Pour in filling.

5. Bake at 450°F for 10 minutes. Reduce oven temperature to 350°F. Bake 35 minutes or until knife inserted in center comes out clean. Cool to room temperature.

6. For garnish, spoon whipped cream around outer edge of pie just before serving. Refrigerate leftover pie.   *Makes 1 (9-inch) pie*

Flute edge or cut small leaves and pumpkins from pastry scraps and press around edge of unbaked pie crust.

Date-Nut Pumpkin Pie

Helpful Hint

To get the most juice from limes, first bring them to room temperature, then roll them around on the counter under the palm of your hand before cutting them in half and squeezing.

Key Lime Tarts

¾ **cup fat-free (skim) milk**
6 **tablespoons fresh lime juice**
2 **tablespoons cornstarch**
½ **cup cholesterol-free egg substitute**
½ **cup reduced-fat sour cream**
12 **packages artificial sweetener** *or* **equivalent of ½ cup sugar**
4 **sheets phyllo dough***
  Butter-flavored nonstick cooking spray
¾ **cup thawed fat-free nondairy whipped topping**

*Cover with damp kitchen towel to prevent dough from drying out.

1. Mix milk, lime juice and cornstarch in medium saucepan. Cook over medium heat 2 to 3 minutes, stirring constantly until thick. Remove from heat.

2. Add egg substitute; whisk constantly for 30 seconds to allow egg substitute to cook. Stir in sour cream and artificial sweetener; cover and refrigerate until cool.

3. Preheat oven to 350°F. Spray 8 (2½-inch) muffin cups with cooking spray; set aside.

4. Place 1 sheet of phyllo dough on cutting board; spray with cooking spray. Top with second sheet of phyllo dough; spray with cooking spray. Top with third sheet of phyllo dough; spray with cooking spray. Top with last sheet; spray with cooking spray.

5. Cut stack of phyllo dough into 8 squares. Gently fit each stacked square into prepared muffin cups; press firmly against bottom and side. Bake 8 to 10 minutes or until golden brown. Carefully remove from muffin cups; cool on wire rack.

6. Divide lime mixture evenly among phyllo cups; top with whipped topping. Garnish with fresh raspberries and lime peel, if desired.   ***Makes 8 servings***

Key Lime Tarts

Summer Fruit Pie

CRUST

1 (9-inch) Classic CRISCO® Double Crust (page 132)

CREAM CHEESE LAYER

4 ounces (half of 8-ounce package) cream cheese, softened

1 egg

2 tablespoons sugar

¼ cup chopped natural or blanched almonds

1 teaspoon all-purpose flour

FRUIT LAYER

¾ cup sugar

¼ cup all-purpose flour

1 can (16 or 17 ounces) pitted Royal Anne or dark sweet cherries packed in heavy or extra heavy syrup, rinsed and drained

2½ cups sliced, peeled freestone peaches (about 1¼ pounds or 5 medium peaches)

1 teaspoon fresh lemon juice

¼ cup almond-flavored liqueur

1. Prepare 9-inch double crust as directed. Roll and press bottom crust into 9-inch Pyrex® pie plate. Do not bake. Heat oven to 400°F.

2. For cream cheese layer, combine cream cheese, egg and 2 tablespoons sugar in small bowl. Mix with spoon until smooth. Stir in nuts. Dust bottom of unbaked pie crust with 1 teaspoon flour. Spread cheese mixture over flour.

3. For fruit layer, combine ¾ cup sugar and ¼ cup flour in small bowl. Sprinkle about one-third of mixture over cheese layer.

4. Combine cherries, peaches and lemon juice in large bowl. Sprinkle remaining sugar mixture over fruit mixture. Toss to coat. Stir in almond-flavored liqueur. Spoon over sugar mixture in pie crust. Moisten pastry edge with water.

5. Cover pie with lattice top, cutting strips 1 inch wide. Flute edge and press with fork.

6. Bake at 400°F for 45 to 50 minutes or until filling in center is bubbly and crust is golden brown. Cool to room temperature before serving. Refrigerate leftovers.   *Makes one 9-inch pie (8 servings)*

Summer Fruit Pie

Cool 'n' Easy® Pie

⅔ **cup boiling water**
1 **package (4-serving size) JELL-O® Brand Gelatin, any flavor**
½ **cup cold water**
   Ice cubes
1 **tub (8 ounces) COOL WHIP® Whipped Topping, thawed**
1 **prepared graham cracker crumb crust (6 ounces)**
   Assorted fruit (optional)

STIR boiling water into gelatin in large bowl 2 minutes or until completely dissolved. Mix cold water and ice to make 1¼ cups. Add to gelatin, stirring until slightly thickened. Remove any remaining ice.

STIR in whipped topping with wire whisk until smooth. Refrigerate 10 to 15 minutes or until mixture is very thick and will mound. Spoon into crust.

REFRIGERATE 4 hours or until firm. Just before serving, garnish with fruit, if desired. Store leftover pie in refrigerator.   *Makes 8 servings*

Banana Cream Pie

1 **9-inch pie crust**
3 **medium bananas**
1 **teaspoon lemon juice**
½ **cup sugar**
6 **tablespoons cornstarch**
¼ **teaspoon salt**
3 **cups fat-free (skim) milk**
2 **egg yolks**
1½ **teaspoons vanilla**
   Nondairy whipped topping (optional)
   Cinnamon and powdered sugar (optional)

Bake pie crust according to package directions; let cool. Slice 2 bananas; toss with lemon juice. Layer in bottom of pie crust.

Combine sugar, cornstarch and salt in medium saucepan. Combine milk and egg yolks; slowly add to dry mixture. Add to medium saucepan and cook over medium heat, stirring constantly until mixture thickens and boils. Boil 1 minute, stirring constantly. Remove from heat, stir in vanilla and pour into pie shell. Immediately cover with waxed paper. Cool. Just before serving remove waxed paper and slice remaining banana. Garnish pie with banana and whipped topping or cinnamon and powdered sugar, if desired.   *Makes 8 servings*

Ginger & Pear Tart

30 gingersnap cookies
½ cup chopped pecans
⅓ cup butter, melted
1 cup sour cream
¾ cup half-and-half
1 package (4-serving size) vanilla instant pudding mix
2 tablespoons apricot brandy
4 ripe pears*
⅓ cup packed dark brown sugar
½ teaspoon ground ginger

Or, substitute 1 (16-ounce) can pear halves, drained and thinly sliced.

Preheat oven to 350°F. Combine gingersnaps and pecans in food processor or blender container; process until finely crushed. Combine crumb mixture and butter in medium bowl. Press firmly onto bottom and up side of 10-inch quiche dish or 9-inch pie plate. Bake 7 minutes; cool completely on wire rack.

Combine sour cream and half-and-half in large bowl. Beat until smooth. Whisk in pudding mix. Add apricot brandy. Beat until smooth. Pour into prepared pie crust. Cover; refrigerate several hours or overnight.

Just before serving, preheat broiler. Peel pears. Cut into thin slices. Arrange in overlapping circles on top of pudding mixture. Combine brown sugar and ginger in small bowl. Sprinkle evenly over pears. Broil 4 to 6 minutes or until sugar is melted and bubbly. (Watch carefully so sugar does not burn.) Serve immediately. **_Makes 6 to 8 servings_**

Tasty Tidbit

If you don't have apricot brandy on hand, beat in an equivalent amount of apricot jam. That way you'll still have the apricot flavor. to complement the pear and ginger flavors.

91

Cranberry Apple Nut Pie

Rich Pie Pastry (page 133)
1 **cup sugar**
3 **tablespoons all-purpose flour**
¼ **teaspoon salt**
4 **cups sliced peeled tart apples (4 large apples)**
2 **cups fresh cranberries**
½ **cup golden raisins**
½ **cup coarsely chopped pecans**
1 **tablespoon grated lemon peel**
2 **tablespoons butter or margarine**
1 **egg, beaten**

Preheat oven to 425°F. Divide pie pastry in half. Roll one half on lightly floured surface to form 13-inch circle. Fit into 9-inch pie plate; trim edges. Reroll scraps and cut into decorative shapes, such as holly leaves and berries, for garnish; set aside.

Combine sugar, flour and salt in large bowl. Stir in apples, cranberries, raisins, pecans and lemon peel; toss well. Spoon fruit mixture into unbaked pie crust. Dot with butter. Roll remaining half of pie pastry on lightly floured surface to form 11-inch circle. Place over filling. Trim and seal edges; flute. Cut 3 slits in center of top crust. Moisten pastry cutouts and decorate as desired. Lightly brush top crust with egg.

Bake 35 to 40 minutes or until apples are tender when pierced with a fork and pastry is golden brown. Cool in pan on wire rack. Serve warm or cool completely. *Makes 1 (9-inch) pie*

Cranberry Apple Nut Pie

PIES

Fruit Tart

⅓ **cup FLEISCHMANN'S® Original Margarine**
1¼ **cups all-purpose flour**
4 **to 5 tablespoons ice water**
1 **cup EGG BEATERS® Healthy Real Egg Substitute**
⅓ **cup sugar**
1 **teaspoon vanilla extract**
1¼ **cups skim milk, scalded**
1 **cup sliced fresh fruit**

In medium bowl, cut margarine into flour until mixture resembles coarse crumbs. Add water, 1 tablespoon at a time, tossing until moistened. Shape into a ball. On floured surface, roll dough into 11-inch circle, about ⅛ inch thick. Place in 9-inch pie plate, making a ½-inch-high fluted edge; set aside.

In medium bowl, combine Egg Beaters, sugar and vanilla; gradually stir in milk. Pour into prepared crust. Bake at 350°F for 45 to 50 minutes or until set. Cool completely on wire rack. Cover; chill until firm, about 2 hours. To serve, top with fruit. *Makes 10 servings*

Prep Time: 30 minutes
Cook Time: 45 minutes

Peanut Butter Cream Pie

¾ **cup powdered sugar**
⅓ **cup creamy peanut butter**
1 **baked (9-inch) pie crust**
1 **cup milk**
1 **cup sour cream**
1 **package (4-serving size) instant French vanilla pudding and pie filling mix**
5 **peanut butter candy cups, divided**
2 **cups thawed nondairy whipped topping**

Combine powdered sugar and peanut butter with fork in medium bowl until blended. Spread evenly in bottom of pie crust.

Place milk and sour cream in large bowl. Add pudding mix. Beat with wire whisk or electric mixer 1 to 2 minutes or until thickened.

Pour half of filling over peanut butter mixture. Coarsely chop 4 candy cups; sprinkle over filling. Top with remaining filling.

Spread whipped topping over filling. Cut remaining candy cup into 8 pieces; place on top of pie. Refrigerate. *Makes 8 servings*

Fruit Tart

HOLIDAYS

Lacy Hearts Cake

2 (8-inch) round cake layers
1 recipe Creamy White Frosting (page 137)
1 recipe Base Frosting (page 136)
    Red cinnamon candies
    Red sugar

SUPPLIES
1 (10-inch) round cake board, covered or cake plate
    Paper doily

1. If cake tops are rounded, trim horizontally with long serrated knife. Place one cake layer on cake board. Spread about ½ cup Creamy White Frosting on cake and top with second cake layer.

2. Frost entire cake with Base Frosting to seal in crumbs; let set. Frost again with remaining Creamy White Frosting. Smooth frosting on top and sides.

3. Cut out heart shape from doily. Place doily heart on cake top about ½ inch from left edge of cake. Place candies around left edge of pattern and about 1½ inches up right side from point, pressing gently into frosting.

4. Carefully lift off doily heart. Reposition doily heart on cake top, fitting left edge of pattern into space of first heart and about ½ inch from right edge of cake. (Be sure bottom points of hearts align.) Place candies around pattern to outline heart.

5. Sprinkle sugar over doily heart so sugar goes through holes, being careful to sprinkle only over doily. Brush sugar through holes in doily with fingertip. Lift off doily heart, being careful to brush any sugar that clings to doily heart inside outlined heart.

6. Position left half of doily heart over left outlined heart and sprinkle with sugar. Lift off doily heart. Use toothpick to remove any sugar outside outlined hearts.

7. For bottom border, place candies around bottom edge of cake, pressing gently into frosting.   *Makes 12 to 16 servings*

Lacy Hearts Cake

Cookie Decorating Party

  1 **can (16 ounces) strawberry frosting, at room temperature**
48 **vanilla wafers or sugar cookies**
¼ to ½ **pound assorted Valentine candies, such as cinnamon hearts, conversation hearts, chocolate candies, red hots and heart-shaped sprinkles**

1. Stir frosting in can until soft and creamy. Divide frosting evenly among small paper cups to equal one paper cup per child.

2. Give each child an equal number of cookies, one paper cup of frosting and assortment of candies. Have children dip cookies into frosting or spread frosting with backs of spoons. Decorate with candies or sprinkles as desired.

Makes 48 cookies

Tip: Use your imagination and create your own decorating party. These cookies are perfect for all holiday and birthday parties. Use different colored frostings, holiday candies and fun sprinkles to create themed cookies for every occasion.

Prep Time: 10 minutes

Conversation Heart Cereal Treats

  2 **tablespoons margarine or butter**
20 **large marshmallows**
  3 **cups frosted oat cereal with marshmallow bits**
12 **large conversation hearts**

1. Line 8- or 9-inch square pan with aluminum foil, leaving 2-inch overhangs on 2 sides. Generously grease or spray with nonstick cooking spray.

2. Melt margarine and marshmallows in medium saucepan over medium heat 3 minutes or until melted and smooth; stir constantly. Remove from heat.

3. Add cereal; stir until completely coated. Spread into prepared pan; press evenly onto bottom using greased rubber spatula. Press candies into top of treats while still warm, evenly spacing to allow 1 candy per bar. Let cool 10 minutes. Using foil overhangs as handles, remove treats from pan. Cut into 12 bars.

Makes 12 bars

Prep and Cook Time: 18 minutes

Cookie Decorating Party

99

Heavenly Oatmeal Hearts

COOKIES

¾ cup Butter Flavor* CRISCO® all-vegetable shortening plus additional for greasing
1¼ cups firmly packed light brown sugar
1 egg
⅓ cup milk
1½ teaspoons vanilla
3 cups quick oats, uncooked
1 cup all-purpose flour
1½ teaspoons cinnamon
½ teaspoon baking soda
½ teaspoon salt
1 cup milk chocolate chips
1 cup white chocolate baking pieces
1 cup honey-roasted peanuts, chopped

DRIZZLE

½ cup milk chocolate chips
½ cup white chocolate baking pieces
1 teaspoon Butter Flavor* CRISCO® all-vegetable shortening

Butter Flavor Crisco® is artificially flavored.

1. Heat oven to 375°F. Grease baking sheets with shortening. Place sheets of foil on countertop for cooling cookies.

2. For cookies, combine ¾ cup shortening, brown sugar, egg, milk and vanilla in large bowl. Beat at medium speed of electric mixer until well blended.

3. Combine oats, flour, cinnamon, baking soda and salt. Mix into creamed mixture at low speed just until blended. Stir in chips, baking pieces and nuts.

4. Place 3-inch heart-shaped cookie cutter on prepared baking sheet. Place ⅓ cup dough inside cutter. Press to edges and level. Remove cutter. Repeat to form remaining cookies, spacing 2½ inches apart.

5. Bake one baking sheet at a time at 375°F for 10 to 12 minutes or until lightly browned. DO NOT OVERBAKE. Cool 2 minutes on baking sheet. Remove cookies to foil to cool completely.

6. For drizzle, place both chips in separate heavy resealable sandwich bags. Add ½ teaspoon shortening to each bag. Seal. Microwave 1 bag at 50% power (MEDIUM). Knead bag after 1 minute. Repeat until mixture is smooth. Repeat with remaining bag. Cut tiny piece off corner of each bag. Squeeze out and drizzle both mixtures over cookies. To serve, cut cookies in half, if desired.

Makes 2½ dozen heart cookies

Shamrock Ice Cream Sandwiches

1 recipe Butter Cookie Dough (page 130)
3 or 4 drops green food color
1 pint ice cream or frozen yogurt, any flavor
SUPPLIES
3½- to 5-inch shamrock-shaped cookie cutter

1. Prepare cookie dough; mix in food color. Cover; refrigerate until firm, about 4 hours or overnight.

2. Preheat oven to 350°F.

3. Roll dough on floured surface to ¼-inch thickness. Cut out cookies using cookie cutter. Place on ungreased cookie sheets.

4. Bake 8 to 10 minutes or until cookies are lightly browned around edges. Remove cookies to wire racks; cool completely.

5. Remove ice cream from freezer; let stand at room temperature to soften slightly, about 10 minutes. Spread 4 to 5 tablespoons ice cream onto flat sides of half of the cookies. Place remaining cookies, flat sides down, on ice cream; press cookies together lightly.

6. Wrap each sandwich in foil; freeze until firm, about 2 hours or overnight.

Makes 6 to 8 cookie sandwiches

Note: *Filled cookies store well up to 1 week in freezer.*

Valentine Ice Cream Sandwiches: *Prepare and chill cookie dough as directed, substituting red food color for green food color. Cut out cookies with heart-shaped cookie cutter. Continue as directed.*

Patriotic Ice Cream Sandwiches: *Prepare and chill cookie dough as directed, substituting red food color for green food color. Cut out cookies with star-shaped cookie cutter. Continue as directed.*

Pumpkin Ice Cream Sandwiches: *Prepare and chill cookie dough as directed, substituting orange food color for green food color. Cut out cookies with pumpkin-shaped cookie cutter. Continue as directed.*

Christmas Tree Ice Cream Sandwiches: *Prepare, tint and chill cookie dough as directed. Cut out cookies with Christmas-tree-shaped cookie cutter. Continue as directed.*

Helpful Hint

To promote even baking and browning when baking cookies, place only one cookie sheet at a time in the center of the oven. If you do use more than one sheet at a time, rotate the cookie sheets from top to bottom halfway through the baking time. If the cookies brown unevenly with just one cookie sheet in the oven, rotate the cookie sheet from front to back halfway through the cooking time.

Festive Easter Cookies

1 cup butter, softened
2 cups powdered sugar
1 egg
2 teaspoons grated lemon peel
1 teaspoon vanilla
3 cups all-purpose flour
½ teaspoon salt
1 recipe Royal Icing (page 138)
Assorted food colors, icings and candies

1. Beat butter and sugar in large bowl at high speed of electric mixer until fluffy. Add egg, lemon peel and vanilla; mix well. Combine flour and salt in medium bowl. Add to butter mixture; mix well.

2. Divide dough into 2 sections. Cover with plastic wrap. Refrigerate 3 hours or overnight.

3. Preheat oven to 375°F. Roll dough on floured surface to ⅛-inch thickness. Cut out cookies using Easter cookie cutters, such as eggs, bunnies and tulips. Place on ungreased cookie sheets.

4. Bake 8 to 12 minutes or just until edges are very lightly browned. Remove to wire racks; cool completely. Prepare Royal Icing. Decorate as desired. Let stand until icing is set. *Makes 4 dozen cookies*

Festive Easter Cookies

Liberty Bell Cake

1 (13×9-inch) cake
1 recipe Creamy White Frosting (page 137)
1 recipe Base Frosting (page 136)
   Blue decorating gel
   Red cinnamon candies

SUPPLIES
1 (19×13-inch) cake board, cut to fit cake if desired, covered
1 (1½-inch) star cookie cutter

1. If cake top is rounded, trim horizontally with long serrated knife. Trim sides of cake. Cut cake as shown in diagram 1 with serrated knife, using ruler as guide.

2. Position pieces on prepared cake board as shown in diagram 2, connecting with some of the Creamy White Frosting.

3. Frost entire cake with Base Frosting to seal in crumbs; let set. Frost again with remaining Creamy White Frosting.

4. Gently press cookie cutter into frosting, leaving imprints as shown in photo. To outline each imprint, hold tip of gel tube just above frosting and gently squeeze tube while guiding tip in straight line over imprint. Stop squeezing, then lift gel tube at end of each star side. Evenly fill in each star with gel.

5. Decorate with candies as shown in photo.   *Makes 16 servings*

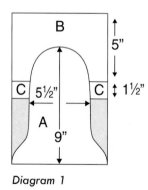

Diagram 1

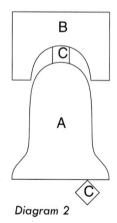

Diagram 2

Helpful Hint

After removing the cake from the oven, let it cool in the pan on a wire rack for about 10 minutes. Loosen it from the side of the pan with a knife or metal spatula. Invert it onto the rack and let it cool completely before cutting or frosting.

Liberty Bell Cake

105

Little Devils

> 1 package (1 pound 2 ounces) carrot cake mix
> ½ cup canned pumpkin
> ⅓ cup vegetable oil
> 3 eggs
> 1 container (16 ounces) cream cheese frosting
> Assorted Halloween candies, jelly beans and chocolate candies

1. Preheat oven to 350°F. Prepare cake mix according to package directions, using water as directed on package, pumpkin, oil and eggs. Spoon batter into 18 paper-lined muffin cups. Bake 20 minutes or until toothpick inserted in centers of cupcakes comes out clean. Cool in pans on wire rack 5 minutes; remove and cool completely.

2. Frost cupcakes with frosting; let each goblin guest decorate his own with assorted candies. *Makes 18 cupcakes*

Jack-O-Lantern

> 2 recipes Buttercream Frosting (page 136)
> 2 (10-inch) Bundt cakes
> 1 recipe Base Frosting (page 136)
> Candy corn

SUPPLIES
> 2 (10-inch) round cake boards, stacked and covered, or large plate
> 1 (6-ounce) paper cup or ice cream wafer cone
> Pastry bag and medium writing tip

1. Tint 4½ cups Buttercream Frosting orange, ½ cup dark green and ¼ cup dark brown.

2. Trim flat sides of cakes. Place one cake on prepared cake board, flat-side up. Frost top of cake with some of the orange frosting. Place second cake, flat-side down, over frosting.

3. Frost entire cake with Base Frosting to seal in crumbs; let set. Frost again with orange frosting.

4. Hold cup over fingers of one hand. Using other hand, frost cup with green frosting. Place upside-down in center of cake to form stem. Touch up frosting, if needed.

5. Using writing tip and brown frosting, pipe eyes and mouth. Arrange candy corn for teeth. Before serving, remove stem. Slice and serve top cake first, then bottom. *Makes 36 to 40 servings*

Little Devils

Boo the Ghost

> 1 (13×9-inch) cake, completely cooled
> 2 cups Light & Fluffy Frosting (page 138)
> 2 black licorice drops or jelly beans

SUPPLIES
> 1 (19×13-inch) cake board, cut in half crosswise and covered
> Plastic spiders (optional)

1. If cake top is rounded, trim horizontally with long serrated knife. Trim sides of cake.

2. Using diagram as guide, draw ghost pattern on 13×9-inch piece of waxed paper. Cut pattern out and place on cake. Cut out ghost. Place on prepared cake board.

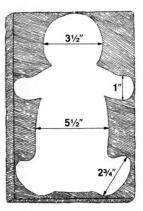

3. Frost ghost, swirling frosting. Arrange licorice drops for eyes and spiders as shown in photo.

Makes 12 to 14 servings

Black Cat Cupcakes

> 1 package (2-layer size) cake mix (any flavor), plus ingredients to prepare mix
> 1 container (16 ounces) chocolate fudge frosting
> Graham crackers
> Black string licorice and assorted candies

1. Preheat oven to 350°F. Line 24 regular-size (2½-inch) muffin pan cups with paper muffin cup liners.

2. Prepare cake mix according to package directions. Spoon batter into prepared muffin pans.

3. Bake 15 to 20 minutes until wooden toothpick inserted into centers comes out clean. Cool in pans on wire racks 10 minutes. Remove to racks; cool completely.

4. Spread tops of cupcakes with frosting. For ears, with serrated knife, carefully cut graham crackers into small triangles; place on cupcakes. Decorate faces with licorice and assorted candies.

Makes 24 cupcakes

Boo the Ghost

Witch Cake

1 package (2-layer size) cake mix (any flavor), plus ingredients to prepare mix
2 containers (16 ounces each) cream cheese or vanilla frosting
  Green paste food color
  Black decorating gel
  Black paste food color
  Red string chewy fruit snacks
1 sugar ice cream cone
  Assorted candies
  Fruit snack roll-up cutouts

SUPPLIES

1 (15×10-inch) cake board, covered, or large tray
  Pastry bag and medium star tip
1 purchased witch's black party hat

1. Preheat oven to 350°F. Grease and flour 13×9-inch baking pan.

2. Prepare cake mix according to package directions; pour batter into prepared pan.

3. Bake 30 to 35 minutes or until wooden toothpick inserted into center comes out clean. Cool in pan on wire rack 10 minutes. Remove from pan to rack; cool completely.

4. If cake top is rounded, trim horizontally with long serrated knife. Place cake on prepared cake board. Spread top and sides of cake with 1 container frosting. Transfer about half of the remaining container of frosting to small bowl; color with green paste food color.

5. Using photo as guide, trace outline of witch's head onto frosted cake with toothpick. Fill in face with thin layer of green frosting; outline with decorating gel as shown in photo.

6. Place remaining frosting in another small bowl; color with black paste food color. Spoon into pastry bag fitted with star tip; pipe frosting around edges of cake.

7. Cut hat in half lengthwise. Place one half on cake; discard remaining half. Unroll string fruit snacks; cut into desired lengths. Place around hat to resemble hair as shown in photo.

8. Place sugar cone on cake for nose. Use candies and fruit snack cutouts to make eyes and mouth as shown in photo. Add black candy to chin for wart.

Makes 12 servings

Witch Cake

Pumpkin Candy Brownies

1 package DUNCAN HINES® Chocolate Lovers Double Fudge Brownie Mix
2 eggs
⅓ cup water
¼ cup vegetable oil
1 cup DUNCAN HINES® Creamy Homestyle Chocolate Frosting
26 pumpkin candies
½ cup DUNCAN HINES® Creamy Homestyle Vanilla Frosting
Green food coloring

1. Preheat oven to 350°F. Line 26 (2-inch) muffin cups with foil liners or place on baking sheets.

2. Combine brownie mix, contents of fudge packet from Mix, eggs, water and oil in large bowl. Stir with spoon until well blended, about 50 strokes. Fill each foil liner with 2 level measuring tablespoons batter. Bake 15 to 17 minutes or until firm. Cool 5 to 10 minutes in pans. Remove to cooling racks.

3. Place Chocolate Frosting in small saucepan. Melt on low heat, stirring constantly. Frost top of 1 warm brownie with generous ½ teaspoonful melted frosting. Top with 1 pumpkin candy; push down slightly. Repeat for remaining brownies. Cool completely.

4. Tint Vanilla Frosting with green food coloring. Place in decorating bag fitted with small leaf tip. Pipe 3 leaves around each pumpkin candy. Use small writing tip to pipe vines, if desired.   ***Makes 26 brownies***

Turkey Cupcakes

- **1 package (2-layer size) cake mix (any flavor), plus ingredients to prepare mix**
- **1 container (16 ounces) chocolate frosting**
- **¾ cup marshmallow creme**
- **24 shortbread ring cookies**
- **2 sticks white spearmint gum**
- **48 small red candies**
- **Assorted candies**

1. Preheat oven to 350°F. Line 24 regular-size (2½-inch) muffin cups with paper muffin cup liners.

2. Prepare cake mix according to package directions. Spoon batter into prepared muffin pans.

3. Bake 15 to 20 minutes or until wooden toothpick inserted into centers comes out clean. Cool in pans on wire racks 10 minutes. Remove to racks; cool completely.

4. Combine frosting and marshmallow creme in medium bowl; mix well. Frost cupcakes lightly with frosting mixture; reserve remaining frosting mixture.

5. Cut cookies in half. Cut half of them in half again to form quarters.

6. For each cupcake, stand larger cookie piece upright on back edge of cupcake for tail. Place 1 of the 2 smaller cookie pieces on opposite side of cupcake for head; discard remaining smaller cookie piece or reserve for another use. Frost cookies with remaining frosting mixture so they blend in with cupcake.

7. Cut gum into ¼-inch pieces; trim both ends of gum into points. Fold gum in half to form beaks; place on bottom edges of heads. Position red candies on heads for eyes. Decorate tops of tails with candies as desired.

Makes 2 dozen cupcakes

Helpful Hint

To easily fill muffin cups, place the batter in a 4-cup glass measure. Fill each cup ¾ full. Use a plastic spatula to control the flow of the batter.

Sugar & Spice Cheesecake

1⅔ cups gingersnap cookie crumbs
⅓ cup butter or margarine, melted
4 packages (8 ounces each) cream cheese, softened
1¼ cups packed brown sugar
3 eggs
1 teaspoon ground cinnamon
1 teaspoon ground nutmeg
½ teaspoon ground cloves
⅓ cup butterscotch-flavored chips
1 teaspoon shortening
Candy corn and assorted candies

1. Preheat oven to 375°F. Combine cookie crumbs and butter in small bowl; mix well. Press evenly onto bottom and 1 inch up side of 9-inch springform pan; set aside.

2. Beat cream cheese in large bowl until fluffy; beat in brown sugar. Add eggs, 1 at a time, beating well after each addition. Blend in spices.

3. Pour batter into prepared crust. Place springform pan on shallow baking sheet. Bake 45 to 55 minutes or until knife inserted into center comes out clean. Cool to room temperature in pan on wire rack. Cover; refrigerate in pan overnight.

4. Using diagram as guide, trace turkey shape onto sheet of foil.

5. Melt butterscotch chips and shortening in small saucepan over low heat, stirring frequently. Spoon onto turkey shape on foil. Immediately place candy corn on tail and decorate turkey with desired candies as shown in photo. Cool completely.

6. With spatula, carefully remove turkey from foil; place on center of cheesecake.

Makes 10 to 12 servings

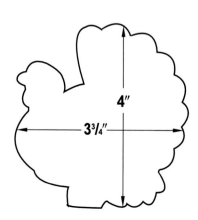

Sugar & Spice Cheesecake

115

Hanukkah Honey Cake

    3 eggs
    ¾ cup packed brown sugar
    ¾ cup vegetable oil
 1¼ cups honey
    ⅔ cup strong coffee
    3 cups all-purpose flour
 1½ teaspoons baking powder
    1 teaspoon baking soda
    ½ teaspoon ground allspice
    ½ teaspoon ground cinnamon
    ½ teaspoon ground nutmeg
    ¾ cup chopped walnuts
 1½ teaspoons grated orange peel
    1 teaspoon grated lemon peel
    2 containers (16 ounces each) vanilla frosting
      Yellow food color

SUPPLIES

    1 (13×9-inch) cake board, covered, or large tray
      Pastry bag and medium writing and star tips
    8 small white candles

1. Preheat oven to 325°F. Grease and flour 13×9-inch baking pan.

2. Beat eggs in large bowl at high speed of electric mixer until thick and lemon colored, about 5 minutes. Beat in brown sugar and oil. Add honey and coffee; stir well. Combine flour, baking powder, baking soda and spices in small bowl; add to batter and stir well. Stir in walnuts and grated peels. Pour into pan.

3. Bake 40 to 45 minutes until cake is golden and toothpick inserted in center comes out clean. Cool in pan on rack 15 minutes. Remove from pan to rack; cool.

4. If cake top is rounded, trim horizontally with long serrated knife. Place cake on prepared cake board. Frost top and sides of cake with 1 container frosting.

5. Using diagram as guide, cut pattern from waxed paper. Place pattern on cake. Trace around pattern with toothpick; remove pattern.

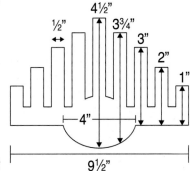

6. Tint remaining container frosting yellow. Spoon into pastry bag fitted with writing tip. Outline menorah with frosting. Using star tip, fill in menorah and pipe border around cake. Insert candles.   *Makes 12 to 14 servings*

Hanukkah Honey Cake

Dreidel Cake

1 package (2-layer size) cake mix, any flavor
1¼ cups water
3 eggs
¾ cup sliced or slivered almonds, toasted and finely ground
¼ cup vegetable oil
½ teaspoon almond extract
1½ containers (16 ounces each) cream cheese frosting
   Yellow and blue food colors

SUPPLIES
1 large tray or (15×10-inch) cake board, covered
   Pastry bag and medium star tip

1. Preheat oven to 350°F. Grease and flour 13×9-inch baking pan.

2. Combine cake mix, water, eggs, almonds, oil and extract in medium bowl. Beat at low speed of electric mixer until blended. Beat at medium speed 2 minutes. Pour batter into prepared pan.

3. Bake 35 to 40 minutes until wooden toothpick inserted into center comes out clean. Cool in pan on wire rack 10 minutes. Remove from pan; cool on rack.

4. If cake top is rounded, trim horizontally with long serrated knife. Cut cake as shown in diagram 1. Position cake pieces on tray as shown in diagram 2, connecting pieces with small amount of frosting. Frost center of cake with about ½ cup white frosting as shown in photo.

5. Tint about ¾ cup frosting yellow. Spread yellow frosting onto top and sides of cake as shown in photo.

6. Using diagram 3 as guide, cut out letter from waxed paper; position on cake as shown in photo. Trace around pattern with toothpick; remove pattern. Tint remaining frosting blue. Spoon frosting into pastry bag fitted with star tip. Use to fill in symbol and pipe around top edge of cake as shown in photo.

Makes 12 servings

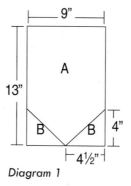

Diagram 1

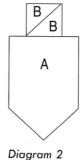

Diagram 2

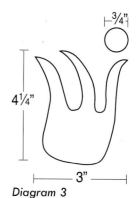

Diagram 3

Dreidel Cake

Candy Cane & Wreath Ornaments

1 cup sugar
½ cup shortening
½ cup butter, softened
1 teaspoon salt
1 egg
2 teaspoons vanilla
2½ cups all-purpose flour
½ teaspoon almond extract
¼ teaspoon liquid green food coloring
¼ teaspoon peppermint extract
½ teaspoon liquid red food coloring, divided
Creamy Decorator's Frosting (page 137)
Assorted red candies

1. Beat sugar, shortening, butter and salt in large bowl with electric mixer at medium speed until light and fluffy. Beat in egg and vanilla until well blended. Beat in flour at low speed until soft dough forms. Remove half of dough from bowl; set aside. Divide remaining dough evenly between 2 medium bowls. Stir almond extract and green food coloring into one portion with wooden spoon until well blended. Stir peppermint extract and ¼ teaspoon red food coloring into remaining portion until well blended.

2. Place level teaspoonfuls of each dough on large baking sheet. Cover; refrigerate 15 minutes or until slightly firm.

3. Preheat oven to 375°F. Place 1 teaspoon red dough, 1 teaspoon green dough and 2 teaspoons uncolored dough on lightly floured surface. Roll out each portion into 6- to 7-inch rope with lightly floured hands. Place 1 green rope next to 1 uncolored rope and 1 red rope next to remaining uncolored rope. Twist each pair of ropes together 7 or 8 times; place on ungreased baking sheet.

4. Shape red and white rope into candy cane and green and white rope into wreath. Repeat with remaining dough.

5. Bake 7 to 9 minutes or until cookies are firm. *Do not allow to brown.* Transfer cookies with spatula to wire racks; cool completely.

6. Prepare Creamy Decorator's Frosting. Tint half of frosting with remaining ¼ teaspoon red liquid food coloring. Spoon frostings into pastry bags fitted with writing tips. Pipe cluster of berries onto wreaths with red frosting. Glue candies onto wreaths with white frosting. Let stand 1 hour or until icing is set. Tie ribbon loops or bows onto each cookie for hanging.

Makes about 4 dozen cookies

Tasty Tidbit

You don't have to wait until the holidays to make these yummy cookies. Color the dough with other colors, make different shapes and enjoy them throughout the year. For example, color half the dough green, leave the remaining half white and twist into shamrock shapes for St. Patrick's Day.

Candy Cane and Wreath Ornaments

121

Snowmen

1 **package (20 ounces) refrigerated chocolate chip cookie dough**
1½ **cups sifted powdered sugar**
2 **tablespoons milk**
   Candy corn, gum drops, chocolate chips, licorice and other assorted small candies

1. Preheat oven to 375°F.

2. Cut dough into 12 equal sections. Divide each section into 3 balls: large, medium and small for each snowman.

3. For each snowman, place 3 balls in row, ¼ inch apart, on ungreased cookie sheet. Repeat with remaining dough.

4. Bake 10 to 12 minutes or until edges are very lightly browned.

5. Cool 4 minutes on cookie sheets. Remove to wire racks; cool completely.

6. Mix powdered sugar and milk in medium bowl until smooth. Pour over cookies. Let cookies stand 20 minutes or until set.

7. Decorate to create faces, hats and arms with assorted candies.

Makes 1 dozen cookies

Pumpkin Jingle Bars

¾ **cup MIRACLE WHIP® Salad Dressing**
1 **two-layer spice cake mix**
1 **(16-ounce) can pumpkin**
3 **eggs**
   Sifted confectioners' sugar
   Vanilla frosting
   Red and green gum drops, sliced

Mix first 4 ingredients in large bowl at medium speed of electric mixer until well blended. Pour into greased 15½×10½×1-inch jelly roll pan. Bake at 350°F, 18 to 20 minutes or until edges pull away from sides of pan. Cool. Sprinkle with sugar. Cut into bars. Decorate with frosting and gum drops.

Makes about 3 dozen bars

Prep Time: 5 minutes
Cook Time: 20 minutes

Snowmen

Candy Cane Cake

1 package DUNCAN HINES® Moist Deluxe® Cake Mix (any flavor)

DECORATOR FROSTING
  5 cups confectioners' sugar
  ¾ cup shortening plus additional for greasing
  ½ cup water
  ⅓ cup non-dairy powdered creamer
  2 teaspoons vanilla extract
  ½ teaspoon salt
    Red food coloring
    Maraschino cherry halves, well drained

1. Preheat oven to 350°F. Grease and flour 13×9×2-inch pan.

2. Prepare, bake and cool cake following package directions for basic recipe. Remove from pan. Freeze cake for ease in handling.

3. For Decorator Frosting, combine confectioners' sugar, shortening, water, non-dairy powdered creamer, vanilla extract and salt in large bowl. Beat at medium speed with electric mixer for 3 minutes. Beat at high speed for 5 minutes. Add more confectioners' sugar to thicken or water to thin frosting as needed. Reserve 2 cups frosting. Tint remaining frosting with red food coloring.

4. Cut frozen cake and arrange as shown. Spread white frosting on cake. Mark candy cane stripes in frosting with tip of knife. Place star tip in decorating bag and fill with red frosting. To make stripes, arrange maraschino cherry halves and pipe red frosting following lines. *Makes 12 to 16 servings*

Tip: For a quick dessert, serve leftover cake pieces with sugared strawberries and dollops of whipped cream.

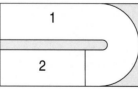

Diagram 1

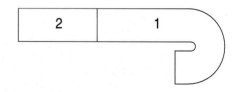

Diagram 2

Helpful Hint

For the best results when baking cakes, avoid opening the oven door during the first half of the baking time. The oven temperature must remain constant in order for the cake to rise properly.

Candy Cane Cake

125

Jolly Peanut Butter Gingerbread Cookies

1⅔ **cups (10-ounce package) REESE'S® Peanut Butter Chips**
¾ **cup (1½ sticks) butter or margarine, softened**
1 **cup packed light brown sugar**
1 **cup dark corn syrup**
2 **eggs**
5 **cups all-purpose flour**
1 **teaspoon baking soda**
½ **teaspoon ground cinnamon**
¼ **teaspoon ground ginger**
¼ **teaspoon salt**

1. Place peanut butter chips in small microwave-safe bowl. Microwave at HIGH (100%) 1 to 2 minutes or until chips are melted when stirred. In large bowl, beat melted peanut butter chips and butter until well blended. Add brown sugar, corn syrup and eggs; beat until light and fluffy. Stir together flour, baking soda, cinnamon, ginger and salt. Add half of flour mixture to butter mixture; beat on low speed of electric mixer until smooth. With wooden spoon, stir in remaining flour mixture until well blended. Divide into thirds; wrap each in plastic wrap. Refrigerate at least 1 hour or until dough is firm enough to roll.

2. Heat oven to 325°F.

3. Roll 1 dough portion at a time to ⅛-inch thickness on lightly floured surface; with floured cookie cutters, cut into holiday shapes. Place on ungreased cookie sheet.

4. Bake 10 to 12 minutes or until set and lightly browned. Cool slightly; remove from cookie sheet to wire rack. Cool completely. Frost and decorate as desired.

Makes about 6 dozen cookies

Jolly Peanut Butter Gingerbread Cookies

Holiday Chocolate Shortbread Cookies

   1 cup (2 sticks) butter, softened
1¼ cups powdered sugar
   1 teaspoon vanilla extract
   ½ cup HERSHEY¡S Dutch Processed Cocoa or HERSHEY¡S Cocoa
1¾ cups all-purpose flour
1⅔ cups (10-ounce package) HERSHEY¡S Premier White Chips

1. Heat oven to 300°F. Beat butter, powdered sugar and vanilla in large bowl until creamy. Add cocoa; beat until well blended. Gradually add flour, stirring until smooth.

2. Roll or pat dough to ¼-inch thickness on lightly floured surface or between 2 pieces of wax paper. Cut into holiday shapes using star, tree, wreath or other cookie cutters. Reroll dough scraps, cutting cookies until dough is used. Place on ungreased cookie sheet.

3. Bake 15 to 20 minutes or just until firm. Immediately place white chips, flat side down, in decorative design on warm cookies. Cool slightly; remove from cookie sheet to wire rack. Cool completely. Store in airtight container.

Makes about 4½ dozen (2-inch diameter) cookies

Note: *For more even baking, place similar shapes and sizes of cookies on same cookie sheet.*

Prep Time: 30 minutes
Bake Time: 15 minutes
Cool Time: 30 minutes

Merry Christmas Present Cake

      Marzipan (page 25)
      Red food color
   1 package (18.25 ounces) devil's food cake mix
   1 cup water
   ½ cup vegetable oil
   3 eggs
   3 tablespoons unsweetened cocoa powder
   1 teaspoon vanilla
   1 cup mini chocolate chips
   ⅔ cup finely ground hazelnuts or almonds
   1 cup whipping cream
   2 tablespoons butter or margarine
   6 ounces semisweet chocolate, coarsely chopped

Prepare Marzipan through step 1. Tint with red food color; set aside. Preheat oven to 350°F. Grease and flour 13×9-inch baking pan. Combine cake mix, water, oil, eggs, cocoa and vanilla in large bowl. Beat with electric mixer at low speed until blended; beat at medium speed 2 minutes. Mix in chocolate chips and nuts. Pour batter into prepared pan. Bake 50 to 60 minutes or until wooden toothpick inserted in center of cake comes out clean. Cool in pan on wire rack 15 minutes. Remove from pan and cool completely on rack.

Bring cream and butter to a simmer in small saucepan; remove from heat. Add chopped chocolate, stirring until melted. Cool to room temperature. Cover; refrigerate until mixture is thick enough to spread, about 1½ hours. Place cake on serving tray. Frost with thickened chocolate mixture. Refrigerate until cake is well chilled, about 2 hours.

Divide Marzipan into 4 equal portions. Roll 1 portion into ½-inch-thick rope. Place rope between sheets of waxed paper and roll into strip 1 inch wide and 16 to 18 inches long (use sharp knife to make edges straight). Lay strip lengthwise down center of cake, continuing down over sides; trim ends to fit. Repeat rolling procedure with second portion of Marzipan; cut crosswise in half. Place strips on cake as shown in Diagram 1; trim ends.

Repeat rolling procedure with third portion of Marzipan, making strip 15 inches long. Fold ends in toward center to make bottom loops of bow; place on cake as shown in Diagram 2. Repeat rolling procedure with fourth portion of Marzipan, making one 8-inch strip and one 4-inch strip. Cut 8-inch strip in half crosswise; fold into 2 loops and place on first loop. Fold under ends of 4-inch strip to form loop; place on second loop as shown in Diagram 2.

Makes 12 to 16 servings

Diagram 2

Diagram 1

BASICS

Butter Cookie Dough

- ¾ **cup butter, softened**
- ¼ **cup granulated sugar**
- ¼ **cup packed light brown sugar**
- 1 **egg yolk**
- 1¾ **cups all-purpose flour**
- ¾ **teaspoon baking powder**
- ⅛ **teaspoon salt**

1. Combine butter, granulated sugar, brown sugar and egg yolk in medium bowl. Add flour, baking powder and salt; mix well.

2. Cover; refrigerate about 4 hours or until firm.

Chocolate Cookie Dough

- 1 **cup butter, softened**
- 1 **cup sugar**
- 1 **egg**
- 1 **teaspoon vanilla**
- 2 **ounces semisweet chocolate, melted**
- 2¼ **cups all-purpose flour**
- 1 **teaspoon baking powder**
- ¼ **teaspoon salt**

1. Beat butter and sugar in large bowl at high speed of electric mixer until fluffy. Beat in egg and vanilla. Add melted chocolate; mix well.

2. Add flour, baking powder and salt; mix well. Cover; refrigerate about 2 hours or until firm.

Christmas Ornament Cookie Dough

2¼ **cups all-purpose flour**
¼ **teaspoon salt**
1 **cup sugar**
¾ **cup butter, softened**
1 **egg**
1 **teaspoon vanilla**
1 **teaspoon almond extract**

1. Combine flour and salt in medium bowl.

2. Beat sugar and butter in large bowl at medium speed of electric mixer until fluffy. Beat in egg, vanilla and almond extract. Gradually add flour mixture. Beat at low speed until well blended.

3. Form dough into 2 discs; wrap in plastic wrap and refrigerate 30 minutes or until firm.

Gingerbread Cookie Dough

½ **cup shortening**
⅓ **cup packed light brown sugar**
¼ **cup dark molasses**
1 **egg white**
½ **teaspoon vanilla**
1½ **cups all-purpose flour**
1 **teaspoon ground cinnamon**
½ **teaspoon baking soda**
½ **teaspoon salt**
½ **teaspoon ground ginger**
¼ **teaspoon baking powder**

1. Beat shortening, brown sugar, molasses, egg white and vanilla in large bowl at high speed of electric mixer until smooth.

2. Combine flour, cinnamon, baking soda, salt, ginger and baking powder in small bowl. Add to shortening mixture; mix well. Cover; refrigerate about 8 hours or until firm.

Classic Crisco® Crust

8-, 9- OR 10-INCH SINGLE CRUST
- 1⅓ **cups all-purpose flour**
- ½ **teaspoon salt**
- ½ **CRISCO® Stick or ½ cup CRISCO® Shortening**
- 3 **tablespoons cold water**

8- OR 9-INCH DOUBLE CRUST
- 2 **cups all-purpose flour**
- 1 **teaspoon salt**
- ¾ **CRISCO® Stick or ¾ cup CRISCO® Shortening**
- 5 **tablespoons cold water**

10-INCH DOUBLE CRUST
- 2⅔ **cups all-purpose flour**
- 1 **teaspoon salt**
- 1 **CRISCO® Stick or 1 cup CRISCO® Shortening**
- 7 to 8 **tablespoons cold water**

1. Spoon flour into measuring cup and level. Mix flour and salt in medium bowl.

2. Cut in shortening using pastry blender (or 2 knives) until all flour is blended to form pea-size chunks.

3. Sprinkle with water, 1 tablespoon at a time. Toss lightly with fork until dough forms a ball.

FOR SINGLE CRUST PIES
1. Press dough between hands to form 5- to 6-inch "pancake." Flour rolling surface and rolling pin lightly. Roll dough into circle.

2. Trim 1 inch larger than upside-down pie plate. Loosen dough carefully.

3. Fold dough in quarters. Unfold; press into pie plate. Fold edge under; flute.

FOR BAKED PIE CRUSTS
1. For recipes using baked pie crust, heat oven to 425°F. Prick bottom and side thoroughly with fork (50 times) to prevent shrinkage.

2. Bake at 425°F for 10 to 15 minutes or until lightly browned.

FOR UNBAKED PIE CRUSTS
1. For recipes using unbaked pie crust, follow baking directions in each recipe.

FOR DOUBLE CRUST PIES
1. Divide dough in half. Roll each half separately. Transfer bottom crust to pie plate. Trim edge even with pie plate.

2. Add desired filling to unbaked pie crust. Moisten pastry edge with water. Lift top crust onto filled pie. Trim ½ inch beyond edge of pie plate. Fold top edge under bottom crust. Flute. Cut slits in top crust to allow steam to escape. Bake according to specific recipe directions.

Reduced-Fat Pie Pastry

1¼ cups all-purpose flour
1 teaspoon EQUAL® FOR RECIPES or 3 packets EQUAL® sweetener or
2 tablespoons EQUAL® SPOONFUL™
¼ teaspoon salt
4 tablespoons cold margarine, cut into pieces
5 to 5½ tablespoons ice water

• Combine flour, Equal® and salt in medium bowl; cut in margarine with pastry blender until mixture resembles coarse crumbs. Mix in water, 1 tablespoon at a time, stirring lightly with fork after each addition until dough is formed. Wrap and refrigerate until ready to use.

• For prebaked crust, roll pastry on lightly floured surface into circle 1 inch larger than inverted 9-inch pie pan. Ease pastry into pan; trim and flute edge. Pierce bottom and side of pastry with fork. Bake in preheated 425°F oven until pastry is browned, 10 to 15 minutes. Cool on wire rack.

Makes pastry for 9-inch pie (8 servings)

Tip: *Double recipe for double crust or lattice pies.*

Rich Pie Pastry

2 cups all-purpose flour
¼ teaspoon salt
6 tablespoons butter
6 tablespoons lard
6 to 8 tablespoons cold water

Combine flour and salt in medium bowl. Cut in butter and lard with pastry blender or 2 knives until mixture resembles coarse crumbs. Sprinkle water, 1 tablespoon at a time, over flour mixture, mixing until flour is moistened. Shape dough into a ball. Roll, fill and bake as recipe directs.

Makes pastry for 1 (9-inch) double pie crust

Note: *For single crust, cut recipe in half.*

Helpful Hint

If pastry or pie dough becomes sticky and difficult to handle, refrigerate it until firm. Then roll out the dough quickly on a lightly floured surface. A tough pie crust is often the result of too much flour worked into the dough or overhandling.

Chocolate Cake

  2 cups sugar
1⅔ cups all-purpose flour
  ½ cup unsweetened cocoa powder
  1 teaspoon baking powder
  ½ teaspoon baking soda
  ¼ teaspoon salt
  1 cup buttermilk
  ½ cup vegetable shortening
  1 teaspoon vanilla
  3 eggs

Preheat oven to 350°F. Grease and flour 2 (8-inch) round or square cake pans or 1 (13×9-inch) cake pan.

Combine sugar, flour, cocoa, baking powder, baking soda and salt in large bowl. Add buttermilk, shortening and vanilla. Beat with electric mixer on low speed 30 seconds or until well blended, scraping side of bowl once. Beat on high speed 2 minutes more, scraping side of bowl occasionally. Add eggs; beat 2 minutes more, scraping bowl once. Pour batter evenly into prepared pans.

Bake 30 to 35 minutes for 8-inch round or square cakes or 35 to 40 minutes for 13×9-inch cake. (Cakes are done when toothpick inserted into centers comes out clean.) Cool in pans on wire racks 10 minutes. Loosen sides of cake layers from pans with knife or metal spatula. Remove to wire racks; cool completely.

Makes 2 (8-inch) round or square cake layers or 1 (13×9-inch) cake

White Cake

2½ cups all-purpose flour
1¾ cups sugar
  3 teaspoons baking powder
  ¼ teaspoon salt
1½ cups milk
  ½ cup vegetable shortening
  2 teaspoons vanilla
  4 egg whites

Preheat oven to 350°F. Grease and flour 2 (8-inch) round or square cake pans or 1 (13×9-inch) cake pan.

Combine flour, sugar, baking powder and salt in large bowl. Add milk, shortening and vanilla. Beat with electric mixer on low speed 30 seconds or until well blended, scraping side of bowl once. Beat on high speed 2 minutes, scraping side of bowl occasionally. Add egg whites; beat 2 minutes more, scraping bowl once. Pour batter evenly into prepared pans.

Bake 30 to 35 minutes for 8-inch round or square cakes or 35 to 40 minutes for 13×9-inch cake. (Cakes are done when toothpick inserted into centers comes out clean.) Cool in pans on wire racks 10 minutes. Loosen sides of cake layers from pans with knife or metal spatula. Remove to wire racks; cool completely.

Makes 2 (8-inch) round or square cake layers or 1 (13 X 9-inch) cake

Yellow Cake

2½ cups all-purpose flour
1¾ cups sugar
2½ teaspoons baking powder
¼ teaspoon salt
1⅓ cups milk
½ cup butter, softened
2 teaspoons vanilla
3 eggs

Preheat oven to 350°F. Grease and flour 2 (8-inch) round or square cake pans or 1 (13×9-inch) cake pan.

Combine flour, sugar, baking powder and salt in large bowl. Add milk, butter and vanilla. Beat with electric mixer on low speed 30 seconds or until well blended, scraping side of bowl once. Beat on high speed 2 minutes more, scraping bowl often. Add eggs; beat 2 minutes more, scraping bowl once. Pour batter evenly into prepared pans.

Bake 30 to 35 minutes for 8-inch round or square cakes or 35 to 40 minutes for 13×9-inch cake. (Cakes are done when toothpick inserted into centers comes out clean.) Cool in pans on wire racks 10 minutes. Loosen sides of cake layers from pans with knife or metal spatula. Remove to wire racks; cool completely.

Makes 2 (8-inch) round or square cake layers or 1 (13 X 9-inch) cake

BASICS

Helpful Hint

When decorating a cake, using a base coat of frosting first seals in the crumbs and makes it easier to get a smooth finished surface. Always let the base coat set for a few minutes before frosting again.

Base Frosting

3 cups powdered sugar, sifted
½ cup vegetable shortening
¼ cup milk
½ teaspoon vanilla
Additional milk

Combine sugar, shortening, ¼ cup milk and vanilla in large bowl. Beat with electric mixer on medium speed until smooth. Add more milk, 1 teaspoon at a time, until frosting is a thin consistency. Use frosting immediately.

Makes about 2 cups

Buttercream Frosting

6 cups powdered sugar, sifted and divided
¾ cup butter or margarine, softened
¼ cup vegetable shortening
6 to 8 tablespoons milk, divided
1 teaspoon vanilla extract

Place 3 cups sugar, butter, shortening, 4 tablespoons milk and vanilla in large bowl. Beat with electric mixer until smooth. Add remaining 3 cups powdered sugar; beat at medium speed until light and fluffy, adding more milk, 1 tablespoon at a time, as needed for good spreading consistency.

Makes about 3½ cups frosting

Chocolate Buttercream Frosting

6 cups powdered sugar, sifted and divided
1 cup butter or margarine, softened
4 to 6 squares (1 ounce each) unsweetened chocolate, melted and cooled slightly
8 to 10 tablespoons milk, divided
1 teaspoon vanilla

Combine 3 cups powdered sugar, butter, melted chocolate to taste, 6 tablespoons milk and vanilla in large bowl. Beat with electric mixer until smooth. Add remaining powdered sugar; beat until light and fluffy, adding more milk, 1 tablespoon at a time, as needed for good spreading consistency.

Makes about 3½ cups

Creamy Decorator's Frosting

1½ cups vegetable shortening
1½ teaspoons lemon, coconut, almond or peppermint extract
7½ cups sifted powdered sugar
⅓ cup milk

Beat shortening and extract in large bowl with electric mixer on medium speed until fluffy. Slowly add half of sugar, ½ cup at a time, beating well after each addition. Beat in milk. Add remaining sugar; beat 1 minute more until smooth and fluffy.* Store in refrigerator. (Frosting may be used for frosting cake and/or piping decorations.)   *Makes about 5 cups*

*If frosting seems too soft for piping roses or other detailed flowers or borders, refrigerate for a few hours. Refrigerating frosting usually gives better results, but you may also try stirring in additional sifted powdered sugar, ¼ cup at a time, until desired consistency.

Creamy White Frosting

½ cup vegetable shortening
6 cups sifted powdered sugar, divided
3 tablespoons milk
2 teaspoons clear vanilla extract
Additional milk*

*For thinner frosting, use more milk and for thicker frosting use less milk.

Beat shortening in large bowl with electric mixer at medium speed until fluffy. Gradually beat in 3 cups sugar until well blended and smooth. Carefully beat in 3 tablespoons milk and vanilla. Gradually beat in remaining 3 cups sugar, adding more milk, 1 teaspoon at a time, as needed for good spreading consistency. Store in refrigerator.   *Makes enough to fill and frost 2 (8-inch) round or square cake layers or frost 1 (13×9-inch) cake*

Helpful Hint

To get bright colors and to keep the frosting at the proper consistency, tint frosting with paste food colors. Add a small amount of the paste color with a toothpick, then stir well. Slowly add more color until the frosting is the desired shade. If you use liquid food colors and the frosting becomes too thin, add additional powdered sugar, beating until the desired consistency is reached.

BASICS

Fudge Frosting

24 large marshmallows, halved
⅔ cup semisweet chocolate chips
½ cup vegetable shortening
½ cup water
5 cups sifted powdered sugar
3 teaspoons vanilla

Place marshmallows, chocolate chips, shortening and water in 1½-quart saucepan. Cook over low heat until melted and smooth, stirring constantly. Remove from heat; let stand 5 minutes. Gradually beat in sugar and vanilla with electric mixer at medium speed about 6 minutes or until mixture starts to lose gloss. Use frosting immediately.

Makes enough to fill and frost 2 (8-inch) round or square cake layers or frost 1 (13×9-inch) cake

Light & Fluffy Frosting

⅔ cup sugar
2 egg whites*
5 tablespoons light corn syrup
Dash salt
1 teaspoon vanilla

*Use only grade A clean, uncracked eggs.

Combine sugar, egg whites, corn syrup and salt in top of double boiler or stainless steel bowl. Set over boiling water. Beat constantly with electric mixer until stiff peaks form, about 7 minutes. Remove from water and beat in vanilla.

Makes about 2 cups

Royal Icing

1 egg white,* at room temperature
2 to 2½ cups sifted powdered sugar
½ teaspoon almond extract

*Use only grade A clean, uncracked egg.

1. Beat egg white in small bowl at high speed of electric mixer until foamy.

2. Gradually add 2 cups powdered sugar and almond extract. Beat at low speed until moistened. Increase mixer speed to high and beat until icing is stiff, adding additional powdered sugar if needed.

ACKNOWLEDGMENTS

The publishers would like to thank the companies and organizations listed below for the use of their recipes and photographs in this publication.

California Prune Board

Duncan Hines® brand is a
    registered trademark of
    Aurora Foods Inc.

Egg Beaters® Healthy Real Egg
    Substitute

Equal® sweetener

Hershey Foods Corporation

Kraft Foods, Inc.

M&M/MARS

The Procter & Gamble Company

USA Rice Federation

Wisconsin Milk Marketing Board

INDEX

METRIC CONVERSION CHART

VOLUME MEASUREMENTS (dry)

⅛ teaspoon	0.5 mL
¼ teaspoon	1 mL
½ teaspoon	2 mL
¾ teaspoon	4 mL
1 teaspoon	5 mL
1 tablespoon	15 mL
2 tablespoons	30 mL
¼ cup	60 mL
⅓ cup	75 mL
½ cup	125 mL
⅔ cup	150 mL
¾ cup	175 mL
1 cup	250 mL
2 cups = 1 pint	500 mL
3 cups	750 mL
4 cups = 1 quart	1 L

VOLUME MEASUREMENTS (fluid)

1 fluid ounce (2 tablespoons)	30 mL
4 fluid ounces (½ cup)	125 mL
8 fluid ounces (1 cup)	250 mL
12 fluid ounces (1½ cups)	375 mL
16 fluid ounces (2 cups)	500 mL

WEIGHTS (mass)

½ ounce	15 g
1 ounce	30 g
3 ounces	90 g
4 ounces	120 g
8 ounces	225 g
10 ounces	285 g
12 ounces	360 g
16 ounces = 1 pound	450 g

DIMENSIONS

1/16 inch	2 mm
⅛ inch	3 mm
¼ inch	6 mm
½ inch	1.5 cm
¾ inch	2 cm
1 inch	2.5 cm

OVEN TEMPERATURES

250°F	120°C
275°F	140°C
300°F	150°C
325°F	160°C
350°F	180°C
375°F	190°C
400°F	200°C
425°F	220°C
450°F	230°C

BAKING PAN SIZES

Utensil	Size in Inches/Quarts	Metric Volume	Size in Centimeters
Baking or Cake Pan (square or rectangular)	8 × 8 × 2	2 L	20 × 20 × 5
	9 × 9 × 2	2.5 L	23 × 23 × 5
	12 × 8 × 2	3 L	30 × 20 × 5
	13 × 9 × 2	3.5 L	33 × 23 × 5
Loaf Pan	8 × 4 × 3	1.5 L	20 × 10 × 7
	9 × 5 × 3	2 L	23 × 13 × 7
Round Layer Cake Pan	8 × 1½	1.2 L	20 × 4
	9 × 1½	1.5 L	23 × 4
Pie Plate	8 × 1¼	750 mL	20 × 3
	9 × 1¼	1 L	23 × 3
Baking Dish or Casserole	1 quart	1 L	—
	1½ quart	1.5 L	—
	2 quart	2 L	—